On The List: 1980s

The 111 Best Music Lists of the 1980s

by Jason Preston

Portions of this book previously appeared on www.goodbadunknown.com

The Good, The Bad, and the Unknown © Jason Preston
Layout and Publishing by Geoff Skinner
Cover Design and Photographs by Kevin Marcus
Edited by Lisa J. Lord

Library of Congress Control Number:
ISBN-13: 978-1731054777
ISBN-10: 1731054777

Dedication

For Hadley & Ellis...
thank you for always letting me take you on trips down my
memory lane

CHAPTERS

INTRODUCTION

I will always remember the first time I heard Guns N' Roses. The moment itself wasn't significant. There wasn't anything crazy happening at the time. I wasn't parachuting out of a plane to Axl Rose's wickedly fierce howl or meeting my true love in the midst of a Slash solo. It was a mundane day and I was doing a mundane thing. It was the summer of '88 and I was taking a high school summer school class. My mom had convinced me to take summer school so I could get that subject out of the way for the school year. Seemed like a great idea, but in retrospect, it wasn't. I still had the same number of classes during the school day. All I did was replace that class with another class that had homework. My point is summer school sucked and Axl Rose saved me.

I don't remember my summer school teacher, I don't remember any of the students, and I don't even remember what class I was taking. I don't remember anything about the class except that it was my introduction to the band that would musically map out the rest of my high school years. During snack break, a couple of kids in the back of the room broke out a small cassette tape player. They popped in what would come to be my musical Holy Grail, *Appetite for Destruction* by Guns N' Roses. Truthfully, from where I was sitting, I could barely hear the music. What I did hear was the discussion about the band. Even my teacher was involved in the discussion. Even he was a fan. The students and my teacher were talking about GN'R like they were the next Led Zeppelin, the next Rolling Stones... they could be bigger than the Beatles. It's hard not to be curious about those endorsements. If someone said they just saw a movie that was better than *Star Wars*, you'd be curious. Even if you

11

hated *Star Wars*, you still would get the cultural significance of that statement. I had to hear this album.

Around that time, my musical tastes circled four main bands: Depeche Mode, The Cure, The Smiths and New Order. They were my fab four. They were the posters on my wall. They were the T-shirts in my closet. They were the cassette tapes on my shelf. I bought a record player just so I could listen to their 12-inch singles that were only available on vinyl. These singles had rare B-sides that could only be heard on a UK or Japanese import. I'm pretty sure I spent almost $20 on Depeche Mode's "Master and Servant" single just to get the B-side, which was an 8-minute version of "(Set Me Free) Remotivate Me." It was worth every penny. Why? It wasn't the music, it was the journey. There was no internet to tell you what singles had rare or unreleased tracks. You had to drive from store to store, looking for an album. The journey could take days, weeks, even months. It was chance and perseverance. But when you found that specific album, you were elated. You felt like you were the one who caught Joe Montana's game-winning pass in the 1982 NFC championship game instead of Dwight Clark. Owning one of those rare vinyl records meant something. It gave you access to the band that no one else had. It made your relationship with your favorite artist more personal. It meant you owned a piece of the band. I wanted to own everything that my favorite bands put out. I wasn't a metal fan at the time. I thought metal was for knuckleheads. After that day in summer school, everything changed. It wasn't just about changing my tastes over what music I liked, but it would change my perception of all music, teaching me to be open to everything.

After summer school, I borrowed my parents Peugeot and headed over to the mall. We had two malls in my town: the Visalia Mall and the Sequoia Mall. The Sequoia Mall had two records stores in it, which were both thin on content. But, the Visalia Mall had a loaded Sam Goody. I went to Sam Goody and searched through the stacks of Grateful Dead tapes (they had a strong local following) only to end up on Hall & Oates. No GN'R. But, this was meant to be. As I was walking out of the store, I noticed a standee advertising newly released albums. Sitting misplaced on top of a stack of Bobby Brown cassettes was one lone cassette for *Appetite For Destruction*. I remember it was Bobby Brown because my brother just purchased that cassette tape a couple of days earlier. He was on a mission to memorize the rap part in the middle of Bobby's song "Every Little Step" (in his defense, he did memorize it). When I brought the GN'R cassette to the counter, the cashier's eyes lit up and he gave me a crooked smile, knowing the life-altering moment I was about to have.

After purchasing the album, I walked straight to my car, pushed the cassette in the stereo and turned it up. The album hit me with such force; I was paralyzed. All I could do was just sit there and listen. I listened to the first three songs before I even had the strength to pull my car out of the parking spot. I had never heard such visceral emotion, such commanding guitars, such honest lyrics. I couldn't stop listening, and I didn't want to.

I lived in a small town. From my house to the mall was a mere six minutes. If I drove straight home, I'd get to hear one more song, maybe two. I wouldn't be able to enjoy this on my bedroom's cheap box stereo. So I didn't go home. I just drove around, listening. In my car, the album thrived like it was alive. I devoured the whole album in one sitting just like the time Theo ate all those hamburgers on *The Cosby Show* (hey, we all liked *The Cosby Show* in the '80s, we didn't know any better, yet).

This was the magical era of the '80s. In one hour, I went from knowing nothing about Guns N' Roses to the band becoming my favorite of all time... that is until 1991. But we will get to that in the next book.

The downright, dirty, filthy sleazy, back alley grit that spewed with such carnal energy out of the speakers is what Guns N' Roses represented to an era that had no limitations. The '80s were a creative Mecca in all forms of media, from music to movies to TV. It was a moment in time when creativity wasn't just cherished, it was a requirement. The only boundaries that existed were the limits of our own imaginations. Anything was possible because we let our imaginations run wild. We took control over what could be accomplished.

One of the best examples of letting our imaginations run free was the glory of the mixtape. A mixtape was a cassette tape that we, the kids of the '80s, made ourselves, featuring our favorite songs. Making mixtapes gave us the power to create soundtracks to our lives. Mixtapes were the modern day playlists. If we were going on a road trip, then Bruce Springsteen and Tom Petty were our guides. If we were going through hard times, we wallowed in Joy Division or Chicago ("Look Away" is a sad song!) If we wanted to dance, we called on Rick James or Kool and the Gang. If we wanted to get the attention of the cutest girl in school, we made her a mixtape with Peter Gabriel or Foreigner (you had to switch it up, depending on the girl).

What ultimately gave mixtapes power was how personal they were. A mixtape was the voice of the person who made it. It didn't just give you a window into the person's soul, but it showed you how passionate they were about making it. Because making a mixtape took effort. Let me tell you.

First, you had to decide on the length of the mixtape. Blank cassette tapes came as short as 30 minutes and as long as 120 minutes. Longer was better, right? Not always. Depending on the purpose, you didn't want it too long. For a road trip, longer was better. But if you were making one as a love note, you had to keep it short, sweet and to the point. Next, you had to find all the songs that you wanted to include. You had to go through each tape you owned and cue it up to the song you wanted to use. Then, you had to sit in front of your stereo and simultaneously hit play on the cassette with the song you wanted and hit record on the blank cassette. Timing was everything. Being off by a half-second was as detrimental as losing a game of tic-tac-toe to the WOPR computer. If you didn't start recording it properly, you might cut off the first few seconds of Prince preaching to his *dearly beloved* or Madonna telling us *we can dance,* which would screw up your seamless flow. Then when it came to the end of the song, you had to stop it at the very second the song ended. If you were one beat too late, then you might end up with a couple of seconds of another song that doesn't fit into the mood that you're trying to create. A few seconds of the abrasive guitar from The Cure's "All I Want" right after their jovial "Just Like Heaven" or the machismo punch of "Pour Some Sugar on Me" after the heart-wrenching destitution of

"Love Bites" had the power to completely decimate the sentiment of an entire mixtape and ruin the experience.

Mixtapes were outlets to our imaginations. There were no rules except for the ones we made for ourselves. We could construct party mixes that included Slick Rick, Billy Squier, Joy Division, Chaka Khan, Cinderella, Kim Carnes, Erasure, EPMD and Rick Springfield all on the same tape. Having so many different genres squeezed onto one mixtape made sense in the '80s because in the '80s nothing went together. That was the point. We were united by this diverse influx of various flavors. Just look at our fashion. We didn't care about matching; we just cared about having fun. Not all of us could be big-time rock stars but making a great mixtape was a pretty close second.

I'm going to let all the non-eighties people in on a secret, everyday life in the '80s sucked. No, really. Don't believe the hype, it was bogus. Our day-to-day lives were very bland. Most of us didn't have a lot. Unemployment was high; wages were low. We feared a nuclear war with Russia on a daily basis. We only had three TV stations; sometimes four if you included PBS. Even cable TV only had 30 channels, if you were rich enough to afford it. That said, having more channels was a curse because if you wanted to change channels, you had to stand up from the couch and walk across the room to do it. We hadn't invented remote controls yet! Our fashion was boring. We wore corduroy pants. Corduroy "cords" were the worst pants ever created because as you were walking in them, they would make a swishing noise that I can only assume is the sound of loneliness. Our cars were slow, uncomfortable, and had elongated radio antennas which were designed to catch obscure AM stations that no one ever listened to. Our world was ordinary. We needed an outlet for our boring lives, so we created fantasy worlds. When we remember the '80s, it's not the everyday lives we reminisce about. We reminisce about the '80s that were created by John Hughes, John Cusack, John Carpenter, Arnold Schwarzenegger, Arnold Jackson, Michael Jackson, Bo Jackson, Bo & Luke Duke, Crockett & Tubbs, K.I.T.T., Pac-Man, Link, Mike Tyson, Steven Spielberg, Steven King, Prince, MTV, Madonna, Soul Train, Spiccoli, Georg Lucas, Sam Malone, the Noid, Indiana Jones, Mario & Luigi, and Guns N' Roses. They were our reality.

We created worlds where cars could travel through time, where golden pirate treasure was hidden somewhere underneath our homes, where ancient demons were causing big trouble in Chinatown. Not only could we be anywhere, we could be anyone. We could be a Jedi wielding the force, we could raise a sword and be the master of the universe, or we could be an out of work plumber trying to rescue our true love back from an angry gorilla. It all made sense by not making sense. Just ask David Byrne. It was the last era before our media surrendered to the influence of accountants and marketing gurus who would mold everything toward its biggest market potential, ripping the soul out of it. We may have been the most eclectic decade, but that's what made it so incredible. We didn't care as much about success as we did about having fun. That is why the '80s have survived. Because at the core of everything we did from yellow heads eating magic dots to computer animated heads selling soda, there was something honest, something true, something human about it. It was as weird as a man turning into a fly, but it was real. At the time of writing this book, a lot of our mainstream media, our TV shows, movies, and music are regurgitated from old ideas and previously successful entities. Accountants have taken over media, pushing creative directions that have the best chance at a financial return. Because of this, today's media isn't personal. Our movies and TV shows don't come from a unique voice, they don't come from a voice at all. They are made in a lab with calculators and spreadsheets. They lack heart, strength, and endurance. *Back To The Future* was released on July 3rd, 1985 and it stayed in the movie theaters until March of 1986... nine months later. When was the last time an original movie did that? Today's media is hollow; it's fabricated, it's processed to be bought and sold. And in the '80s, if we knew anything, we knew that true happiness was not bought, processed or sold.

The music of the '80s championed the decade's sense of wonder. New genres flourished, from goth to metal to rap to alternative to even the beginnings of electronica; the '80s would give birth to more new genres than any other decade. These genres took chances. They pushed music in new directions. They tried things that never should have worked but did. Bobby McFerrin had a number one hit with no instruments ("Don't Worry Be Happy"). Even as we pushed boundaries as far as they would bend, our music at its core was authentic. The songs, the lyrics, the passion was rooted in real human sentiment. And even if you stripped away all the keyboards and computerized production, you were left with a song that had real heart to connect with its audience in a long-lasting way.

This book is a look back at a truly magical era through the bands that helped shape it. Each list is made up by me. There is no hard or fast rule to why some songs are ranked higher than others, or why some songs are included and others are not. While I included some big radio hits, radio hits are not always a band's best offering, they're just the most commercial. These lists are windows back in time. They are snapshots, mixtapes of an era. They are meant to be conversation starters, doorway drugs, avenues back in time for those of us who were there to relive some of the best musical moments of that decade. Also, it's to introduce new fans to what we enjoyed. There are many, many bands that could have been included in this book, the selections here are reflective of my own '80s favorites or experiences.

The only rules for the book was for any band to be included, they had to have released at least three full-length albums during the decade. For the songs, they had to be released at some point in the eighties. So when you wonder why Joan Jett's "I Love Rock N' Roll" doesn't make her list, now you know why...though it was popular in the '80s, it came out in the '70s. Ultimately, this book is about fun. Read it with a keyboard tie, a Jolt cola, and a boombox and I promise that you'll have so much fun that you'll want to phone home about it.

*   *   *

THE 111 BEST ALBUMS OF THE DECADE

In creating the top 111 best albums, it comes down to finding albums that were not only great, but also helped define the musical landscape of the decade. Though some of my favorites have slipped in here (it's my book), a majority of the albums were important in the musical legacy of the era.

The 111 Best Albums of the '80s:

1. **The Cure** - *Disintegration* (1989) - This atmospheric masterpiece is the perfect dark horse contender for album of the decade. The songs are so rich with complexity, repeat listens don't even do it justice. It's a hypnotic journey through a chaotic range of emotions, expanding from depression to love. It was the zenith of alternative music. This is the album that all other alternative albums would be forever measured up to, challenging the pop norm with the grace and poetic artistry of a modern rock opera.

2. **Guns N' Roses** - *Appetite For Destruction* (1987) - The album that made Axl, Slash, Duff, Izzy and Steven household names. *Appetite* practically oozes the filth of the Hollywood underbelly with its gritty, rambunctious, sleaze-infested grooves. It is literally an album about sex, drugs, and rock n' roll. And it's one of the best ever made.

3. **Prince** - *Purple Rain* (1984) - Prince's concept album (and rock-laced film) is the career apex of one of rock's all-time greatest songwriters. With sexy charisma, sprinkled with the euphoria from a party that never ends, it is the type of album that can only be made by an icon as legendary as his purple majesty.

4. **U2** - *War* (1983) - With a rebel yell, U2's album started their revolutionary war. It was a brazen battle cry against war, tyranny, and suppression. In a never-ending, ground-breaking career, this is their most passionate effort.

5. **Michael Jackson** - *Thriller* (1982) - This is pop perfection by the aptly crowned king of pop. Who knew a video of dancing zombies could be so much fun?

6. **AC/DC** - *Back in Black* (1980) - After losing their singer, Bon Scott, during early production, this album had everything going against it. Instead, it became the hardest rocking album the world had ever known. It set the high bar and continued to shake us all decade long.

7. **The Clash** - *London Calling* (1980) - Though released in the UK in very late 1979, it wasn't released in the US until 1980. The album's impact and influence spread throughout the '80s like an adrenaline shot to rock's DNA. It is the album that every punk album aspires to be. It is the album that every punk band aspires to deliver. It is the album every punk worships like scripture.

8. **N.W.A.** - *Straight Outta Compton* (1988) - As hip-hop emerged this decade, N.W.A. took it by the reigns with an angry fist thrust into the air. They exposed a part of America that mainstream society had been blissfully ignoring for too long. The words of N.W.A. hit with such honesty that the world had no choice but to stand up and take notice.

9. **Tom Petty** - *Full Moon Fever* (1989) - This is technically Petty's first solo album, but it could be considered a supergroup. The album features most of Petty's backing band (the Heartbreakers), two Beatles (though Ringo only shows up in the video), 4/5 of the Traveling Wilburys and a song-stealing cameo by Del Shannon. It is an album overflowing with pure Americana. It runs down like a dream.

10. **The Beastie Boys** - *Paul's Boutique* (1989) - There were so many samples used on this ground-breaking hip-hop album that there were entire websites dedicated to dissecting every song snippet used. This album's song sampling was so far ahead of its time, we still have years to go to catch up.

11. **R.E.M.** - *Life's Rich Pageant* (1986) - As modern rock simmered under the surface of the mainstream, R.E.M. was the genre's work horse. On this album, the boys from Athens, GA, created the ultimate college rock album that you didn't need a fake ID to buy.

12. **Bruce Springsteen** - *Nebraska* (1982) - Bruce's everyman story-telling peels back the layers of blue-collar America, revealing an intimate portrait of the

citizens and the destructive challenges that plague their desolate lives. Who knew being born in the US would be so bleak but sound so good?

13. **Public Enemy** - *It Takes A Nation Of Millions* (1988) - If they gave out college degrees in rap skills, Chuck D would be a Ph.D. for every single course. Meanwhile, his partner in rhyme, Flava Flav, would be throwing the best parties on campus.

14. **The Police** - *Synchronicity* (1983) - With their final release as a band, the Police shed their reggae influence replacing it with emotionally-laced spiritual vibes. Inspired by the author, Arthur Koestler, the band added a new layer of depth to their lyrics and songwriting, creating their most potent, successful album of their career.

15. **The Smiths** - *Queen Is Dead* (1986) - Morrissey's signature croon led a legion of alienated youth through lyrics smothered in sarcasm and wit, with a tongue-in-cheek delivery as if everyone was in on the joke. Morrissey may have been the only one laughing, if he even knows how to laugh.

16. **Run DMC** - *King Of Rock* (1985) - There is no doubt that this bombastic rap trio are the kings of the genre, and to this day sucka MCs still call them Sire.

17. **Prince** - *1999* (1982) - There is a heated debate among fans whether this album is actually a better album than *Purple Rain*. The songs dive deeper into musical composition while layering complex melodies that are delivered in an explosive poptastic way. *Purple*

Rain is more historically relevant, but *1999* is musically superior.

18. **U2** - *The Joshua Tree* (1987) - U2 pushed their visionary scope to the limits on this sweeping effort. It was so successful, their music videos provided MTV with more content than all of the seasons of *Remote Control* combined.

19. **Van Halen** - *1984* (1984) - The band hated each other during the recording of this album. David Lee Roth thought he was the world's best singer. Eddie Van Halen thought he was the world's best guitar player. Alex Van Halen thought he was the world's best drummer. And bassist Michael Anthony was just happy to be there.

20. **Jane's Addiction** - *Nothing's Shocking* (1988) - This alternative rock album is an eclectic patchwork of songs, brilliantly woven together into a magnificent cabinet of curiosities. It is the trail-blazing grandfather to the Lollapalooza culture that would dominate the '90s and beyond.

21. **Boogie Down Productions** - *Criminal Minded* (1987) - With their lead street prophet, KRS-One, bringing his brand of rhymin', rhymin', rhymin' to the masses, this album put the New York rap scene on the map, making it the center of the East Coast hip-hop empire.

22. **Bruce Springsteen** - *Born In The USA* (1984) - As the reigning working-class champ, Bruce delivered a message of support for all the disenfranchised hard-working Americans who didn't feel like they had a

voice. With seven Top 10 singles, their sentiments finally had an audience.

23. **Talking Heads** - *Remain In Light* (1980) - The Heads expand their sonic limits by drawing on the influences of world music from Jamaican reggae, Haitian percussion, and Nigerian polyrhythm; creating their magnum opus.

24. **Joy Division** - *Closer* (1980) - The dark intimacy and stark inner reflection is brought forth with such light it embraces you with its heart and soul. The last album before singer Ian Curtis' tragic death is a snapshot of a life of depression, searching for hope.

25. **Hüsker Dü -** *Zen Arcade* (1984) – This punk rock concept album follows a punk rock kid looking for solace in a non-punk rock world; it includes songs rooted in jazz, folk, and pop. It's the most non-punk rock, punk rock album to infiltrate the impressionable ears of America's youth.

26. **The Beastie Boys** - *Licensed To Ill* (1986) - Here's a little album I got to tell about three bad brothers that we know so well. It started way back in the *eigh-ties* with Adrock, MCA and he, Mike D.

27. **The Pixies** - *Surfer Rosa* (1988) - Before the '90s when alternative rock took over the mainstream, a little band called the Pixies broke ground on not just a sound but a movement. The album was too raw to be rock but too gigantic to be punk. It was The Pixies at their best.

28. **Metallica** - *...And Justice For All* (1988) - The Rocky Balboa of hard rock. The mount Olympus of thrash.

Metal's gold standard (or in Metallica's case... black gold). In this outing, the band takes a progressive approach, churning out mile-long songs executed at breakneck speeds resulting in head-banging delirium.

29. **R.E.M.** - *Murmur* (1983) - The band's debut album is a rumbling mumble that hit like a thunderstorm. They shook the current rock clichés of the day to create something with enough passion to talk about.

30. **Depeche Mode** - *Black Celebration* (1986) - On this album, Depeche Mode transitioned from their Eurodisco dance to the darker melodies and deeper introspection that would eventually become the siren song to teenagers everywhere, dressed in black.

31. **Peter Gabriel** - *So* (1986) - Be warned, listening to this album may cause you to stand outside your true love's window holding a boombox over your head.

32. **The Replacements** - *Tim* (1985) - Paul Westerberg and company are in full swing party mode, creating one of the most gratifying rock albums of the decade and a college rock staple for all times.

33. **The Cars** - *Heartbeat City* (1984) - If you want to go back in time to glimpse what life was like in the '80s, you need to go no farther than the Andy Warhol directed video for the Cars' track, "Hello Again." Was Warhol a genius, who captured the perfect snapshot of an era, or were the Cars so tapped into the time, they brought it out in him? Maybe it's just magic.

34. **Run-DMC** - *Raising Hell* (1986) - This album spread throughout every household in America until all of

the citizens were rhyming, wearing Adidas, and eating at Kentucky Fried.

35. **New Order** - *Low-Life* (1985) - On this album, New Order finally shed the last bit of atmosphere from their previous incarnation as Joy Division and solidified their movement into a dance hall staple with substance.

36. **Mötley Crüe** - *Too Fast For Love* (1981) - Before glam metal covered the planet in its hairspray, Mötley Crüe debuted with an album so raw and gritty, it sounded like an indie rock album made in the garage by a group of high school slackers. But there was no slack on this lean, mean, party machine.

37. **Michael Jackson** - *Bad* (1987) - The album sold 10 million copies and still paled in comparison to its predecessor, *Thriller*. Granted, every album in history pales in comparison to *Thriller*. Rick Springfield's entire catalog pales in comparison to *Thriller*. *Bad* was an epic effort, producing five number one singles and nine hit music videos. In this case, second best is still a smooth thrill.

38. **Eric B & Rakim** - *Paid In Full* (1987) - Rakim's unique skillful rhyming was awe-inspiring while Eric B's production became the instruction manual for sampling in hip-hop. This album wasn't just ground-breaking, it was the album that laid the ground to break.

39. **Kraftwerk** - *Computer World* (1981) - Kraftwerk's eerie examination of the rise of the computer is an honest, bleak, yet accurate look at the electronic future.

While the message is a future skimmed of its human emotion, the music is still fun to listen to.

40. **The Pretenders** - *The Pretenders* (1980) - For eons, rock music had been dominated by men. Then the Pretenders emerged led by the tenacious wit and cold hard truths spouted by the chiseled voice of Chrissie Hynde. Her voice was powered by such raw confidence, Hynde sang like she had a pair of brass balls in her pocket.

41. **Janet Jackson** - *Rhythm Nation 1814* (1989) - With seven top ten singles and four number ones, this socially conscious concept album, is as revolutionary as it is a dancing machine.

42. **U2** - *The Unforgettable Fire* (1984) - This album so clearly represents American pride in such an accurate and personal way, it's head-scratching that it was created by four wee lads from Ireland.

43. **Roxy Music** - *Avalon* (1982) - The band's last album as a group is a fitting culmination of their lustrous career, finding Bryan Ferry and company settling into a smoother groove as they bring down the final curtain. There will never be anything more than this.

44. **Judas Priest** - *British Steel* (1980) - They didn't just break the law with this one, they broke all the rules. Judas Priest is "The" metal God of all heavy metal that would dominate the '80s.

45. **John Lennon & Yoko Ono** - *Double Fantasy* (1980) - This is the best thing to come out of the union of John and Yoko (sorry, Sean). Though it doesn't make up for Yoko breaking up the Beatles, it's a touching

collection of songs by a couple who truly loved each other despite society's disdain for them.

46. **Prince** - *Dirty Mind* (1980) - While most of artists would be subtle in their approach to sexual innuendos in their songs, Prince produced an album of songs that literally hit the nail right on the head. Prince was singing about incest decades before *Game of Thrones* made it cool.

47. **INXS** - *Kick* (1987) - Though the album wasn't a critical success, the fans came out in droves in support of this effort by the Australian lads. MTV dominance gave this album all the credit and Moonman statues it deserved.

48. **Marvin Gaye** - *Midnight Love* (1982) - The final studio album released before the death of the most soulful voice the world has ever known. It was Gaye's first album away from Motown, breathing new life into his career as it drew on current styles and trends, even bringing synthpop and new wave into the mix.

49. **de la Soul** - *3 Feet High And Rising* (1989) - Bucking the trend of their contemporaries, reflecting on the gravity of street life, de la Soul put out an album that emitted a positive glow, as a celebration of life. From nursery rhymes to Hall & Oates samples, de la was the magic number.

50. **Nine Inch Nails** - *Pretty Hate Machine* (1989) - With a cannon of riff-heavy songs, Nine Inch Nails distanced themselves from their rival industrial music contemporaries without hesitation. Trent Reznor wrote and recorded most of the songs on the album

while he was down in it working as a janitor. No wonder he has so much anger.

51. **Bruce Springsteen** - *The River* (1980) - It's an uncompromising journey through the heartland of America. It traverses through the lives and cities that make up the backbone of the country. No one captures the aching soul of America with more honesty than Bruce.

52. **Iron Maiden** - *Number Of The Beast* (1982) - Mixed in the deeper levels of hell in the blackest of all cauldrons, is this savage concoction of metal-grinding guitars, seismic-inducing drums, and blood-curdling screams. It's the perfect storm of demonic evil coupled with pure head-banging goodness.

53. **LL Cool J** - *Radio* (1985) - LL spit rhymes with so much carnal energy and machismo, muscle-bound men stayed away from the beach for years just in case Cool James decided to stop by.

54. **The Stone Roses** - *The Stone Roses* (1989) - It defined Britpop before Britpop was defined. The album was largely ignored upon its release. It wasn't until years later, that its influence and appreciation have solidly stood the test of time.

55. **Tears For Fears** - *Songs From The Big Chair* (1985) - The album that dragged new wave out of the dark, back alley club and planted it firmly at center stage of the biggest arenas. You didn't need to shout to know that everybody in the world was head over heels for Tears for Fears.

56. **Pixies** - *Doolittle* (1989) - Here comes your Pixies as they doomore on their second release, building their grumbling rhythmic noise into mainstream acceptance.

57. **Fine Young Cannibals** - *The Raw & The Cooked* (1988) - If you were to take all the '80s one-hit wonders, throw them in a blender and mix them into a perfect blend of pop sensibilities, the Fine Young Cannibals would be the result. Every song on this album is so flawlessly crafted, it drives the listener crazy with what a good thing it is.

58. **The Clash** - *Combat Rock* (1982) - In an effort to capture the energy and angst of their early days, this became the last Clash album to feature the classic line-up while exemplifying everything the band is, was, and will ever be.

59. **Metallica** - *Kill 'Em All* (1983) - Riding the blitzkrieg assault of thrashing guitars, growling vocals, and pure aggression, Metallica's debut album landed with such intense force that it sought and destroyed all other metal bands in the way.

60. **Depeche Mode** - *Music For The Masses* (1987) - Nothing compares to the strange journey of Depeche Mode. This album brought the band to the masses, culminating in an epic sold-out performance at the Rose Bowl, a feat very few bands before them were able to do.

61. **Pet Shop Boys** - *Actually* (1987) - On their second album, instead of the typical bubblegum pop we expected, the band went political, criticizing the rule

of then-British Prime Minister, Margaret Thatcher. While they were asking her what the people had done to deserve it, we were asking what we had done to deserve such a fantastic album.

62. **Yazoo** - *Upstairs at Eric's* (1982) - In between his brief stint with Depeche Mode and his career with Erasure, Vince Clarke teamed with Alison Moyet to create a magical snapshot of early '80s synthpop. Drawing upon the digital love of Kraftwerk, the duo created an album that was as ambitious as it was accessible. Also, it's loved by mannequins everywhere.

63. **The Traveling Wilburys** - *Volume 1* (1988) - Bob Dylan, George Harrison, Tom Petty, Jeff Lynne, and Roy Orbison walk into a recording studio. Do you really need any more than that?

64. **Madonna** - *Like A Prayer* (1989) - Was she talking about God or was she talking about her lover? Oh, wait, I get it now...

65. **Morrissey** - *Viva Hate* (1988) - His first solo outing after the break-up of the Smiths is a confident, strident statement. Moz is more than a voice, he is a creative entity. *Viva Hate* embodies the best of the Smiths, while kindly warning all hairdressers to keep a fire extinguisher nearby.

66. **Janet Jackson** - *Control* (1986) - Legendary producers Jimmy Jam and Terry Lewis took the baby sister of the Jackson family and turned her into an iconic feminist leader. With five top ten singles, Janet didn't just take control of her career, she took control over the charts.

67. **Soft Cell** - *Non-Stop Erotic Cabaret* (1981) - It's a sleazy, naughty roller coaster ride through every club you've ever dreamed of sneaking into but never having the courage to actually make it happen. Bring your dancing shoes, moustaches encouraged.

68. **Joan Jett** - *Bad Reputation* (1981) - With classic '50s swagger, rebellious '60s rock, and angry '70s punk, Jett made the coolest album to rock a leather jacket.

69. **New Order** - *Brotherhood* (1986) - My favorite album of the 80s is the direct middle ground between what Joy Division was and what New Order would ultimately become. Holding onto the grounded character of the British post-punk era while elevating the energy with pulse-pounding BPMs, New Order delivers their most personal album.

70. **Lionel Richie** - *Can't Slow Down* (1983) - Richie brought it all on this one. With the hip-shaking funk of the Commodores and soulful, gut-wrenching ballads, *Can't Slow Down* erupted into an international sensation. We weren't just dancing on the ceiling, we were dancing on every wall in the house... all night long.

71. **The Replacements** - *Let It Be* (1984) - It was the first album where the band stopped wailing on their instruments as loud as possible and started writing actual songs. It's a post-punk rock favorite thing and one of the cornerstones of alternative rock.

72. **Talk Talk** - *Spirit of Eden* (1988) - It's the spirit of improvisational jazz that pulsates through the veins of this conceptual album, reinventing the band's

creative direction. At the time, the album was largely dismissed but has gone to be a major influence to bands like Blur, Sigur Ros, and Radiohead.

73. **Missing Persons** - *Spring Session M* (1982) - The destination was unknown with the release of this new wave club thumper. Dale Bozzio's unmistakable squeak is as alluring as it is defiant.

74. **DEVO** - *Freedom of Choice* (1980) - Heavily influenced by literary imagination and political sarcasm, Devo's move into peppy synthpop is a deeply enjoyable tongue-in-cheek affair that you can whip a stick at.

75. **The Fall** - *This Nation's Saving Grace* (1985) - The Fall's style of taking everything, mashing it in a punk blender, and spitting it out in a bombastic array of fuzzy guitars and grungy vocals is exactly what we needed.

76. **Sonic Youth** - *Daydream Nation* (1988) - Before teenage angst paid off well, there was a teenage riot trashing up the underground music scene. Below modern rock, below punk, a fury of guitars was gestating into this sonic boom that hit our audio lobes with an onslaught of finely tuned feedback.

77. **Oingo Boingo** - *Dead Man's Party* (1985) - Though it happened in the movie *Weird Science*, this album will not give you the power to create a girl out of a magazine for you. But, like the movie, it will make you the life of the party.

78. **Human League** - *Dare!* (1981) - After losing two founding members to the Heaven 17 spin-off, the band ditched their avant-garde approach for straight

up commercial pop and the cover of Vogue magazine. It's an album that celebrates the simple pleasures of life, and gives us great music that dreams are made of.

79. **Prince** - *Sign O' The Times* (1987) - 2 create an album w/1 pristinely produced song after another is only possible in the 2 capable hands of a musical genius.

80. **Faith No More** - *The Real Thing* (1989) - Introducing Mike Patton's unparalleled vocal range (six octaves!), Faith No More came from out of nowhere to bridge the gap between the riff-heavy metal music of the '80s and the grind of '90s grunge rock. An epic album that appealed to everyone, unless you were a fish.

81. **Stevie Wonder** - *Hotter Than July* (1980) - On his nineteenth album, Wonder finally scores his first official platinum record. That wasn't enough for Stevie. He used the album's popularity as a springboard to persuade the country to establish January 15th as national Martin Luther King, Jr. Day.

82. **Echo & The Bunnymen** - *Crocodiles* (1980) - The debut album by these dark and moody hooligans is a frenzied whirlwind of chanting guitars, blended bass, and the most sultry voice this side of Las Vegas.

83. **The Smiths** - *Meat Is Murder* (1985) - Ignited by the head-spinning dizziness from the song "How Soon Is Now?" and Morrissey's passionate howl, this might be the first album to go vegan.

84. **Journey** - *Escape* (1981) - Journey sheds their progressive rock roots and fully embraces arena rock. The album is one long Steve Perry solo, howling at

his vocal zenith. This album is so incredible, cities built arenas just to have Journey come and play in them. I don't know if that's true, but it sounds good.

85. **The Cure** - *Kiss Me Kiss Me Kiss Me* (1987) - Before we were hit with *Disintegration*'s epic mystical scope, we were taken on a Dante-like quest through the darker corners of Robert Smith's psyche. *Kiss Me* (x3) is a patchwork of a band uncovering new roads, exploring new places and reaching deep into what their souls have to bare.

86. **The Minutemen** - *Double Nickels on the Dime* (1984) - Inspired by Hüsker Dü's *Zen Arcade*, this is the Minutemen's *Moby Dick*, *Hamlet* and *Oedipus Rex*. It's a treasure chest of what punk rock can do when you stop thinking like a punk rock band.

87. **Duran Duran** - *Rio* (1982) - Duran Duran didn't need to save a prayer for the hungry jubilance that shines on this record. Simon Le Bon's suave would become the new religion as Duran Duran catapulted to '80s rock Gods.

88. **Minor Threat** - *Discography* (1989) - I may be cheating with this one. Though it's technically a compilation of their previous EPs and singles, it's the only complete cohesive album this punk ensemble ever put out. Minor Threat was so potent, they could only last for one album. It's a pivotal moment in time, so powerful, it still resonates today.

89. **Whitney Houston** - *Whitney* (1987) - After twenty million in sales, Whitney had no problem finding somebody to dance with.

90. **Tom Petty** - *Hard Promises* (1981) - With his Southern swagger and his signature Florida grin, Petty fought to keep his promises to his fans and took on his record company. Petty refused to release this album if they raised the album price for customers. Petty stood his ground and won for fans everywhere.

91. **Fleetwood Mac** - *Tango In The Night* (1987) - The last studio album by the band's most popular line-up before their chaotic later years would redefine the band over and over. It's a wonderful swan song with the band smartly incorporating the '80s synth sound without giving up their blues backbone.

92. **Black Flag** - *Damaged* (1981) - No one thought punk could get more aggressive after the '70s rebellion. No one, except Henry Rollins. *Damaged* is the punk album that other punk albums don't want to run into in a dark alley. Don't let its reputation dissuade you, it's also the punk album that rises above all others.

93. **U2** - *Boy* (1980) - This may not even be one of U2's top three albums, but this brilliant debut is better than most bands' greatest efforts.

94. **Afrika Bambaataa** - *Planet Rock* (1986) - If there was a blueprint for how rap renegades get funky, this would be the flagship.

95. **The Dream Syndicate** - *The Days of Wine and Roses* (1982) - Layered with counter-culture wit, this debut is the most New York sounding album to come out of California. Paisley shirt: optional.

96. **Bauhaus** - *In The Flat Field* (1980) - If Bela Lugosi was still alive, the odds are he would be a fan of this dark

entry. As the first Goth record ever, this is the album that established the fashion trend for monochromatic teens across the country.

97. **Tracy Chapman** - *Tracy Chapman* (1988) - Somehow Tracy Chapman hopped out of a time-traveling phone booth from the '60s to deliver this authentic folk album, stripped bare of any '80s narcissism or pretensions. In a time when we needed more to have more, Chapman did more with less.

98. **The Police** - *Zenyatta Mondatta* (1980) - Despite the critical acclaim, the recording of this album was a struggle and the result was roundly hated by the band. Sting even burned a copy of Andy Summers' demo for "Behind My Camel" because of how much he detested it. Luckily, Sting doesn't work for the Recording Academy.

99. **Rush** - *Moving Pictures* (1981) - A modern day masterpiece. Mean, mean stride. Rush's *Moving Pictures*. Listen, listen... all right...

100. **The English Beat** - *I Just Can't Stop It* (1980) - Dave Wakeling and Ranking Roger's moment in the sun is this ska-tastic, dance institution. Play this album to blow the roof off of any house party or to stimulate any beach bonanza.

101. **Bad Brains** - *I Against I* (1986) - This cornerstone of Jah-loving, American punk sent rippling inspirations through our culture like shelves full of unsolved Rubik's Cubes. It reached so far into our zeitgeist, the teen TV show, *Degrassi* named an episode after it.

102. **Jesus and Mary Chain** - *Psychocandy* (1985) - This dirge-fest is every bit basement-dwelling garage rock as it is candy-coated psychedelic hippie rock. Grab some 'shrooms and strap in.

103. **Slick Rick** - *The Great Adventures of Slick Rick* (1988) - Slick Rick's fun-loving stroll through the neighborhoods of his youth are filled with astute proverbs for the best of life and the most unusual.

104. **Dead Kennedys** - *Fresh Fruit For Rotting Vegetables* (1980) - These American punks were as political as they wanted to be, from holidays in foreign lands to the most uber leaders California has ever seen. Lead singer, Jello Biafra's nasally yodel is the beckoning siren to revolution.

105. **Red Hot Chili Peppers** - *Mother's Milk* (1989) - On the first album featuring the band's new line-up (which would be their most successful), the Peppers refine their funk-based jams into velocity-driven rock songs to reach higher ground.

106. **R.E.M.** - *Document* (1987) - R.E.M. steps over the Mason-Dixon line and spreads their Southern grumble to the rest of America. With the band's first love song and a song warning about the end of the world, we felt fine and we knew it.

107. **Stevie Nicks** - *Bella Donna* (1981) - Stevie's debut solo album away from Fleetwood Mac, should really be called Stevie Nicks and the Heartbreakers. With Tom Petty's influential shadow all over this one, Stevie proved she was a brilliant songbird in her own right.

108. **David Bowie** - *Let's Dance* (1983) - Yes, David Bowie, our red shoes are on, so we're ready for the blues.

109. **Big Daddy Kane** - *It's A Big Daddy Thing* (1989) - Kane branches out with a big album for a big personality,   but where this succeeds is when Kane sheds his tough guy image for a glimpse at his sensitive side. There's pimpin', too.

110. **Howard Jones** - *Dream Into Action* (1985) - If happiness could be found on a cassette tape, you would be hard-pressed to find a better candidate than Howard Jones' bright outlook on life even when it sucks. The '80s had a lot of manufactured plastic pop; Jones' brand of personal pop rose above it.

111. **Nirvana** - *Bleach* (1989) - Before *Nevermind* would dominate the '90s and forever, the band's first album crept in at the tail end of the decade with a grunge punk awareness too far ahead of its time to get noticed. It would take their 1991 breakout success for this album to get the recognition it deserves. Years later it holds up as the perfect transition between the radio-driven pop song riffs of the '80s and the guitar-driven noise rock of the '90s.

A FLOCK OF SEAGULLS

In the '80s, if you wanted to watch a TV show, you had to be home at the exact time the show was on to see it. Supposedly, you could program your VHS or Betamax to record the show, but I don't know anyone who successfully did it. Programming a VCR was harder than programming MS-DOS. Even if you managed to get your VCR to record something, half the time you ended up recording the wrong show. Nothing was worse than recording *Cheers* and getting *She's the Sheriff* instead. Therefore, watching shows became an event. Staying home to watch *Miami Vice* was the place to be. The lifestyle of the characters Crockett & Tubbs was the ultimate American fantasy of cool clothes, fast cars, mansions and beautiful women. Even if the characters didn't own shaving cream, they owned Lamborghinis, which is why we wanted to be them.

While *Miami Vice* was the quintessential '80s TV show, A Flock of Seagulls' song, "I Ran" was the quintessential '80s song. With space age melodies fluttering through the speakers like digital doves, a driving beat that sounded like the soundtrack to a late-night car race, and a crooning front man guiding you into a world of fast fashion, A Flock of Seagulls became the sound of a generation. "I Ran" was a rejection of the '60s generation, who fought to change the world. We wanted to embrace life and enjoy the luxuries it had to offer. That's what *Miami Vice* and A Flock of Seagulls gave us: pure guilt-free enjoyment.

Albums of the '80s:

A Flock of Seagulls (1982)

Listen (1983)

Story of a Young Heart (1984)

Dream Come True (1985)

The 11 Best Songs By A Flock of Seagulls:

1. **I Ran** (*A Flock of Seagulls*)
2. **Space Age Love Song** (*A Flock of Seagulls*)
3. **Messages** (*A Flock of Seagulls*)
4. **Wishing I Had A Photograph** (*Listen*)
5. **Nightmares** (*Listen*)
6. **The More You Live The More You Love** (*The Story of A Young Heart*)
7. **The End** (*The Story of A Young Heart*)
8. **Over The Border** (*Listen*)
9. **The Traveler** (*Listen*)
10. **The Story of A Young Heart** (*The Story of A Young Heart*)
11. **You Can Run** (*A Flock of Seagulls*)

Fun Fact: Lead singer, Mike Score, and bassist, Frank Maudsley were both hairdressers before starting the band. They created the band's signature hairstyles to represent a seagull in flight.

A-HA

A-ha's video for "Take On Me" may be the most definitive '80s video of all the definitive '80s videos. The story follows the adventures a woman who is prone to dining and dashing, that falls in love with a fictional character in a comic book. After "Tronning" herself into the comic book, she and the cartoon man of her dreams ogle each other through a magic window that transforms comic book characters into real people and real people into comic book characters. Still with me? The symbolism in the video is a perfect analogy to the entire state of pop culture in the '80s. Music videos were the secret ingredient for success in the battle for chart supremacy. The visual counterpart to any song had to elevate the song's existence. In the '80s, we obsessed over the two-dimensional characters on screens. We dreamed of falling into the TV and roving around Michael Jackson's illuminated sidewalk or the Beastie Boys' house parties. Music videos made musicians into visual entities. Bands were no longer isolated voices that sprang from a transistor radio; they were real people we could admire, worship and fall in love with. It would be oversimplifying to call the 80s a superficial decade, but it would be ignorant to pretend that we were anything else. Style was king. "Take On Me" is the video that exemplified our society. It was the dream that the two-dimensional characters on the screen were only an out-reached hand away. That life was universally better on the other side of the TV screen.

Albums of the '80s:

Hunting High and Low (1985)
Scoundrel Days (1986)
Stay On These Roads (1988)

The 11 Best Songs By A-Ha:

1. **Take On Me** (*Hunting High And Low*)
2. **The Sun Always Shines On TV** (*Hunting High And Low*)
3. **Out Of Blue Comes Green** (*Stay On These Roads*)
4. **Blue Sky** (*Hunting High And Low*)
5. **I've Been Losing You** (*Scoundrel Days*)
6. **Hunting High And Low** (*Hunting High And Low*)
7. **The Living Daylights** (*Stay On These Roads*)
8. **Stay On These Roads** (*Stay On These Roads*)
9. **Scoundrel Days** (*Scoundrel Days*)
10. **Train Of Thought** (*Hunting High And Low*)
11. **The Weight Of The Wind** (*Scoundrel Days*)

Fun Fact: A-ha's video for "Take On Me" won six MTV video music awards, which was twice as many Moonman statues than Michael Jackson won for "Thriller."

Song Note (Take On Me): The song was originally titled, "The Juicy Fruit Song."

AC/DC

AC/DC has the greatest story in all of rock n' roll. In the '70s, they were just a small hard rock band from Australia. Even though they hadn't reached mainstream popularity, many people championed the band as the next big thing. That was until the lead singer, Bon Scott, died suddenly in 1979, during the recording of their new album. The future of the band looked bleak. The band auditioned many singers but couldn't find anyone that fit AC/DC's musical style. As they were debating "breaking up", the band found Brit Brian Johnson from the glam band Geordie. Even with the electric power of Johnson's voice, no one thought he could replace the frenetic energy of Bon Scott. Fans and critics counted them out. Until...

Back in Black was AC/DC's first album with Brian Johnson as the lead singer and it was an explosive album unlike any rock album that came before it. The album hit like lightning and struck like thunder. It became rock radio's mandatory playlist staple and the measuring stick for every rock album to come after it. If AC/DC got a dime for every time I listened to "Shook Me All Night Long" while cruising in high school, the band would be millionaires from that alone. But they didn't need my help as the album would go on to sell 50 million copies and become the 2nd highest selling album of all time in the world. Second only to Michael Jackson's *Thriller.*

Albums of the '80s:

Back in Black (1980)
For Those About To Rock We Salute You (1981)
Flick of the Switch (1983)
Fly On The Wall (1985)
Blow Up Your Video (1988)

The 11 Best Songs By AC/DC:

1. **You Shook Me All Night Long** (*Back In Black*)
2. **Back in Black** (*Back In Black*)
3. **Who Made Who** (*Who Made Who*)
4. **For Those About To Rock (We Salute You)** (*For Those About to Rock*)
5. **Shoot To Thrill** (*Back In Black*)
6. **Shake Your Foundations** (*Fly On The Wall*)
7. **Heatseeker** (*Blow Up Your Video*)
8. **Evil Walks** (*For Those About to Rock*)
9. **Hells Bells** (*Back In Black*)
10. **Two's Up** (Blow Up Your Video)
11. **Bedlam in Belgium** (Flick of the Switch)

Fun Fact: Bon Scott was the first person to discover Brian Johnson. Scott loved how Johnson would writhe around on stage while performing live. The band hired Johnson because of his live stage presence. Turns out, the night Scott saw Johnson perform, Johnson was writhing on stage due to a burst appendix.

BRYAN ADAMS

Coming of age teen movies came of age in the '80s. John Hughes movies were the rage, but it was Cameron Crowe who first peeled back the hunky-dory view of high school with *Fast Times at Ridgemont High*. Studios tried to veer into the college space, but they had less success. Everyone knows college kids are trouble, so there was no veneer to rub off. A few college movies did crack through but only when led by untraditional college students. *Back to School* starred Rodney Dangerfield as an adult heading back to college, while *Real Genius* featured a high school age genius heading to campus. The most significant moment in *Real Genius* is when our high school hero meets the girl of his dreams at a wild party, while "One Night Love Affair" by Bryan Adams plays in the background. Like many '80s movies, pivotal movie moments were coupled with pop songs; and, this moment had the perfect combination. The song enhanced the scene as much as the movie enhanced the song. The song and the moment are forever fused together in my brain (just like at the end of the movie when Tears For Fears became forever fused with Jiffy Pop). Like Rodney, Bryan was a rocker who never got any respect but does deserve his due. In *Real Genius*, the big genius on campus faces being replaced by a younger version of himself. This happened to Bryan in the 2000s when a similar solo artist with almost the exact same name arrived on the scene. Luckily, the music world isn't like college. Bryan and his replacement get along. I mean, when was the last time two musical artists had a beef?

Albums of the '80s:

Bryan Adams (1980)
You Want It You Got It (1981)
Cuts Like A Knife (1983)
Reckless (1984)
Into The Fire (1987)

The 11 Best Songs By Bryan Adams:

1. **One Night Love Affair** (*Reckless*)
2. **Run To You** (*Reckless*)
3. **Summer of '69** (*Reckless*)
4. **Hidin' From Love** (*Bryan Adams*)
5. **Remember** (*Bryan Adams*)
6. **Lonely Nights** (*You Want It You Got It*)
7. **Wastin' Time** (*Bryan Adams*)
8. **Somebody** (*Reckless*)
9. **This Time** (*Cuts Like A Knife*)
10. **Hearts on Fire** (*Into The Fire*)
11. **Heaven** (*Reckless*)

Fun Fact: Bryan Adams originally signed to A&M records for one dollar.

Song Note (Run To You): Bryan originally wrote the song for the band Blue Öyster Cult, but the BÖC rejected it, so Bryan recorded it himself. The song became Adams' biggest hit at the time.

AEROSMITH

Run D.M.C. & Aerosmith's video for "Walk This Way" is one of the decade's most pivotal moments in music. It represents the moment when hip-hop took the reins to main stream radio from classic rock. With rock n' roll legend Aerosmith opening the doorway for the future Godfathers of rap with Run D.M.C., this moment not only transcended music it upended culture. By combining forces, the video launched both Run D.M.C.'s career and resurrected Aerosmith's. Aerosmith ruled in the 70s, but at the beginning of the 80s, they were floundering. Guitarists Joe Perry and Brad Whitford had left the band prior to the album, *Rock In A Hard Place*, which failed to strike. Even when Perry and Whitford returned for the next album, *Done With Mirrors*, the reception was tepid at best. With poor critical reviews and minor radio play, these were the first two albums of the band's career that didn't go platinum. Then in July 1986, Run D.M.C. released their reinterpretation of Aerosmith's classic "Walk This Way" and overnight, Tyler and the boys were back in the saddle. Aerosmith's next two albums (*Permanent Vacation* and *Pump*) would go on to sell over 12 million copies combined. The band would end the decade with another pivotal music video, the David Fincher directed "Janie's Got a Gun." Due to the graphic subject matter of child abuse, it was one of the first MTV videos to come with a warning. By embracing rap and tackling controversial subjects, Aerosmith endured and proved to everyone that they were still the fine risk takers and trailblazers they had always been.

Albums of the '80s:

Rock In A Hard Place (1982)
Done With Mirrors (1985)
Permanent Vacation (1987)
Pump (1989)

The 11 Best Songs By The Aerosmith:

1. **Janie's Got A Gun** (*Pump*)
2. **Angel** (*Permanent Vacation*)
3. **Magic Touch** (*Permanent Vacation*)
4. **Lightning Strikes** (*Rock In A Hard Place*)
5. **The Other Side** (*Pump*)
6. **F.I.N.E.** (*Pump*)
7. **Gypsy Boots** (*Done With Mirrors*)
8. **What It Takes** (*Pump*)
9. **Hoodoo/Voodoo Medicine Man** (*Pump*)
10. **Rag Doll** (*Permanent Vacation*)
11. **Darkness** (*Done With Mirrors*)

Fun Fact: Steven Tyler was eating a batch of French fries at the Anchorage restaurant in New Hampshire. They were the best fries Tyler had ever eaten and he asked to meet the chef. The chef was Joe Perry. Perry was not excited. It turns out Tyler always left a big mess after eating and Perry was the one who cleaned up after him. This is how Steven Tyler and Joe Perry met.

BAD BRAINS

As a kid, I lived under the fear of nuclear war with Russia. The Cold War may have been a silent behind-the-scenes battle, but it left its citizens with an anxiety-provoking uncertainty that we all could be wiped off of the planet at any moment. Even movies like *The Day After*, which followed society after a nuclear war, were best-case scenarios but those best-case scenarios were so hellish, they would give Freddy Krueger night sweats. The '80s had one real glimpse at what nuclear war could be like. In 1986, a reactor at the Chernobyl nuclear power plant in Russia suffered a complete meltdown, spewing radiation into the air like the fireworks at a Kiss concert. It rendered over 20 square miles unlivable, spread its contamination over 150,000 square miles, and killed thousands. This reactor failure pales in comparison to what a nuclear explosion would do, and it still changed the landscape forever.

Bad Brains were the nuclear bomb of the D.C. punk scene. They hit with such power and velocity that they wiped out anyone within their vicinity. Bad Brains pulled musical influences from jazz, funk, and reggae, and were so exotically unique, you were eagerly drawn into hearing what they would do next. Bad Brains laid the foundations for hardcore punk. Hardcore punk wasn't just louder and faster; it was layered with more complex arrangements. By adding complexity to their songs, Bad Brains transformed punk into a genre that could transcend the musical landscape.

Albums of the '80s:

Bad Brains (1982)
Rock For Light (1983)
I Against I (1986)
Quickness (1989)

The 11 Best Songs By Bad Brains:

1. **I Against I** (*I Against I*)
2. **Banned In DC** (*Bad Brains*)
3. **I** (*Bad Brains*)
4. **Rock For Light** (*Rock For Light*)
5. **Big Takeover** (*Bad Brains*)
6. **At The Movies** (*Rock For Light*)
7. **Sailin' On** (*Bad Brains*)
8. **I and I Survive** (*Rock For Light*)
9. **We Will Not** (*Rock For Light*)
10. **House of Suffering** (*I Against I*)
11. **The Prophet's Eye** (*Quickness*)

Fun Fact: The band's live shows were so intense, violent, and destructive, that the band was banned in their hometown of Washington D.C. by every club owner in the city.

Song Note (Sacred Love): Lead singer, H.R., recorded the vocals for this track over the phone while serving time in prison for a cannabis charge.

BAUHAUS

Explaining the world of Goth is like navigating a Halloween maze while on drugs, blindfolded in the dark. It's a murky swamp of emotionally damaged lyrics that are enticing as they are fearful. There's a romantic allure to creeping up to the edge of the sinkhole of death and peering into the great empty void. Though other bands may be more popular for carrying the goth flag, Bauhaus is the genre's Ren MacCormick, dancing gloriously across the macabre cemetery of life. Bauhaus is the band that pried open that cobweb-filled attic and exposed their soul to the disaffected few, who felt that no one out there understood them. Bauhaus understood, and they embraced that disenfranchisement and wore it as a badge of honor (next to about 50 buttons of other bands they liked). They celebrated the aspects of life where others wallowed, and they wallowed where others grasped superficial joy. They didn't glamorize death; they respected it. Death cannot exist without life. And no life escapes death. Instead of running from the inevitable, Bauhaus tries to understand it and ultimately, why does it need to exist? Because without death, there would be no Bauhaus. What makes Bauhaus the champions of the alienated youth, is their respect for depression. Pretending that pretty love songs are going to make it rain flowers and unicorns is an illusion. Life can be a black cloud that some people can't escape, and Bauhaus gave them light by letting those affected know that they are not alone in the dark.

Albums of the '80s:

In The Flat Field (1980)

Mask (1981)

The Sky's Gone Out (1982)

Burning From The Inside (1983)

The 11 Best Songs By The Bauhaus:

1. **In The Flat Field** (*In The Flat Field*)
2. **Dark Entries** (Single)
3. **Doubledare** (*In The Flat Field*)
4. **Lagartija Nick** (*Lagartija Nick Single*)
5. **Passion of Lovers** (*Mask*)
6. **She's In Parties** (*Burning From The Inside*)
7. **Stigmata Martyr** (*In The Flat Field*)
8. **Who Killed Mr. Moonlight?** (*Burning From The Inside*)
9. **Dancing** (*Mask*)
10. **Honeymoon Croon** (*Burning From The Inside*)
11. **Ziggy Stardust** (*Ziggy Stardust Single*)

Fun Fact: After seeing Bauhaus perform live, director Tony Scott hired them to be in his movie about vampires. Bauhaus can be seen performing the song "Bela Lugosi's Dead" in the opening scene of the 1983 movie *The Hunger*, starring David Bowie and Susan Sarandon.

PAT BENATAR

In the '80s, we were obsessed with how we looked. To look good, we had to get in shape. Working-out was as much of a fad as acid-wash jeans or fanny packs. From Jazzercise to Suzanne Somers' interest in our thighs, every week there was a new exercise craze that swept the country. Whether it was Jane Fonda's work-out video or Richard Simmons sweatin' to the oldies, no work-out was complete unless you were blasting music. When I was a kid, I had a summer school teacher who made us do aerobics every morning. She thought she was hip because she played us popular songs from the radio. Her favorite artist was Pat Benatar. Every morning, she started the work-out with Pat Benatar's "Hit Me With Your Best Shot." As part of the work-out, she made us act it out. We did the routine so much that it is ingrained in my psyche. I can still do it today. Yep, just tried it, still remember every move. Pat Benatar connected with her audience on a personal level. She sang for the woman who was stuck in a bad relationship, she sang for the woman who was stuck in a bad job, she sang for the woman who deserved better in life but was always getting the short end of the stick. Pat Benatar wasn't their counselor; she was their cheerleader. Her songs instilled confidence in women, encouraging them that they could accomplish anything. She challenged them to go out there and take it. It wasn't just love that was a battlefield; it was all of life.

Albums of the '80s:

Crimes of Passion (1980)
Precious Time (1981)
Get Nervous (1982)
Seven The Hard Way (1985)
Wide Awake In Dreamland (1988)

The 11 Best Songs By Pat Benatar:

1. **Invincible** (*Seven The Hard Way*)
2. **Anxiety** (*Get Nervous*)
3. **Love Is A Battlefield** (*Live From Earth*)
4. **Fire And Ice** (*Precious Time*)
5. **Hit Me With Your Best Shot** (*Crimes of Passion*)
6. **Tell It To Her** (*Get Nervous*)
7. **The Victim** (*Get Nervous*)
8. **Treat Me Right** (*Crimes of Passion*)
9. **Sex As A Weapon** (*Seven The Hard Way*)
10. **We Belong** (*Tropico*)
11. **Promises In The Dark** (*Precious Time*)

Fun Fact: In 2001, Pat Benatar was a guest star on the television show, *Family Law*, appearing in the episode, "Recovery." One of the writers on that episode was me (Jason Preston).

Song Note (Love Is Battlefield): When Benatar's label first heard the song, they hated it and refused to release it. Benatar battled with them for months to convince them it belonged. The song was a huge hit and went to #5 on the charts.

BLACK FLAG

Black Flag's punk presence belted our ears like a baseball bat smashing a Top 40 jukebox until it was obliterated and any memory of it was wiped permanently from our minds. All the while, Henry Rollins had his boot heel firmly planted on the neck of the roller skating disco mania, staring it down with an icy cold glare of a serial killer sizing up his next victim. Black Flag was the beacon of anarchy, the purveyor of rebellion, the sound of defiance. You have to be at school? You have a pretty girlfriend? That's a new suit? Rollins and Greg Ginn didn't give a shit. They would take it all from you with the sheer force of Rollins' voice busting open your eardrum and Ginn's guitar melting your brain. If there was a superhero with a super voice, Rollins would beat the crap out of him and bury him in a ditch. Then, he'd eat half your lunch and throw the rest away, just to be a dick. Henry Rollins may be the angriest singer to ever bellow into a microphone. In real life, Rollins happens to be one of the kindest, nicest, and smartest rock stars I've ever met. I was lucky enough to have a conversation with him at a book fair when I was in college. He was nothing like the crazed tyrant he played on stage but had more in common with college professors on our campus. Ironically, one of the professors who taught at my school was Greg Graffin (singer of Bad Religion). Maybe punk rock singers and college professors are more alike than we thought. Besides, who wouldn't want a college degree from the University of Rollins?

Albums of the '80s:

Damaged (1981)
My War (1984)
Family Man (1984)
Slip It In (1984)
Loose Nut (1985)
In My Head (1985)

The 11 Best Songs By Black Flag:

1. **Rise Above** (*Damaged*)
2. **Damaged II** (*Damaged*)
3. **Drinking and Driving** (*In My Head*)
4. **Gimme Gimme Gimme** (*Damaged*)
5. **American Waste** (*Six Pack*)
6. **Jealous Again** (*Jealous Again*)
7. **The Bars** (*Slip It In*)
8. **TV Party** (*Damaged*)
9. **Beat My Head Against The Wall** (*My War*)
10. **Black Coffee** (*Slip It In*)
11. **Slip It In** (*Slip It In*)

Fun Fact: Black Flag's symbol of four black bars is their interpretation of a black flag of anarchy. If a white flag represents surrender, then their flag represents the opposite.

BON JOVI

In the '00s, Jon Bon Jovi said that Steve Jobs was to blame for killing the record store. He has a point. In the 2000s, iTunes made buying music so easy that people stopped browsing for music in stores. In the '80s, the record store was king. Buying music was as much an experience as it was listening to it. Every time you went to a record store to buy an album, you flipped through the other releases by that artist (and any other artists near them in the alphabet). You became familiarized with other releases. You may have went to buy Janet Jackson's *Control,* but the spooky looking Siamese twins on the cover of Jane's Addiction's *Nothing Shocking* intrigued you. That doesn't happen anymore. We only know what we want, and we only want what we know. Buying albums based on cover artwork is gone. We've forgotten how important cover artwork is... or was. Seeing the cover art for an album in a record store was a visual advertisement for that album. Like Peter Gabriel's melting face, Prince on his motorcycle, or Bruce Springsteen leaning in a doorway, hands in his pockets, staring at you; album covers were our artwork. Maybe this is why Bon Jovi and the other '80s bands have lasted so long. They came from an era where bands built foundations with fans who took the time to hunt down their music. When you can buy music from your cell phone, there's no connection to it. There's no journey. Without a connection, there's nothing holding the fan base in place. Bon Jovi has always appreciated its fans, and it's why their fans will always want them dead or alive.

Albums of the '80s:

Bon Jovi (1984)

7800 Fahrenheit (1985)

Slippery When Wet (1986)

New Jersey (1988)

The 11 Best Songs By Bon Jovi:

1. **Livin' On A Prayer** (*Slippery When Wet*)
2. **Runaway** (*Bon Jovi*)
3. **Born To Be My Baby** (*New Jersey*)
4. **Price of Love** (*7800 Fahrenheit*)
5. **Shot Through The Heart** (*Bon Jovi*)
6. **Breakout** (*Bon Jovi*)
7. **I'd Die For You** (*Slippery When Wet*)
8. **Wild Is the Wind** (*New Jersey*)
9. **Only Lonely** (*7800 Fahrenheit*)
10. **You Give Love A Bad Name** (*Slippery When Wet*)
11. **Burning For Love** (*Bon Jovi*)

Fun Fact: Jon Bon Jovi's (Bongiovi) first recording gig was singing on the song "R2-D2, We Wish You A Merry Christmas" for the Star Wars Christmas album, *Christmas in the Stars.*

Song Note (You Give Love A Bad Name): The song was originally written for the band Loverboy, but after hearing it, Jon and Richie Sambora decided to keep it for themselves.

BOOGIE DOWN PRODUCTIONS

The '80s loved their MTV. It was our Bible. We spent hours watching Martha Quinn and JJ Jackson tell us what artists we should be listening to. We didn't just want our MTV; we wanted music with us at all times. That's why we had: the boombox. A boombox was a large portable stereo that you could carry with you anywhere. All you had to do was hoist it on your shoulder and turn up the volume so anyone within a 10-block radius could hear the newest beat by Kool Moe Dee. You were doing society a favor by playing songs they didn't know they wanted to hear. Before the cataclysm of Napster, the boombox was the only way to share music.

Rap music owes its popularity to the boombox. The boombox wasn't just a way to listen to music; it was a lifestyle. You were judged by the size of your box, and bigger was always better. Rap is defined by its bravado. It isn't just about what is being said; it's about the confidence in how it is said. Boogie Down Productions spit rebellious social raps with an intense passion rarely seen in any genre of music. Their grim portrayal of inner-city poverty and crime was a rally cry for the community, assuring them that they were in this together. KRS-One's lyrics flowed off his tongue with natural poetic harmony, like a beat poet inciting an audience at a Jesse Jackson rally to tear down the political infrastructure. But anarchy came at a cost. Most radio stations avoided controversy and wouldn't play rap. Rap needed a new avenue. The boombox was rap's soapbox.

Albums of the '80s:

Criminal Minded (1987)
By All Means Necessary (1988)
Ghetto Music: The Blueprint of Hip Hop (1989)

The 11 Best Songs By Boogie Down Productions:

1. **Criminal Minded** (*Criminal Minded*)
2. **My Philosophy** (*By All Means Necessary*)
3. **9mm Goes Bang** (*Criminal Minded*)
4. **You Must Learn** (*Ghetto Music*)
5. **South Bronx** (*Criminal Minded*)
6. **The Bridge Is Over** (*Criminal Minded*)
7. **I'm Still #1** (*By All Means Necessary*)
8. **The Blueprint** (*Ghetto Music*)
9. **Dope Beat** (*Criminal Minded*)
10. **Ya Slippin'** (*By All Means Necessary*)
11. **Why Is That?** (*Ghetto Music*)

Fun Fact: When KRS-One was featured on the cover of their debut album brandishing a gun, critics accused him of encouraging violence. In reality, the gun was a symbol of protection from the true criminals in society, the rich and elite, the real people who were keeping their communities impoverished.

DAVID BOWIE

Childhood was not complete in the '80s without the valiant help of Jim Henson. Henson, who created the *Muppet Show*, brought his Muppets to the big screen in the with numerous sequels (okay, just two). He created the Muppet 2.0 TV show, *Fraggle Rock*. He created Yoda...yes, he created Yoda from *Star Wars*. He also created the fantasy film, *The Dark Crystal*, which starred all puppets. Off the success of *The Dark Crystal*, Henson was hired to direct his first movie, called *Labyrinth*. Unlike *The Dark Crystal*, *Labyrinth* starred a human girl traveling through a world of puppets on her way to see the Goblin King, played by the chameleon-like starman, David Bowie. *Labyrinth* was not as successful at the box office as *The Dark Crystal* and it was considered by many to be a flop. Years down the road, both films have retained a cult following, but it's *Labyrinth* that has endured. While *The Dark Crystal* is considered a kids movie, Bowie brought an air of maturity to *Labyrinth*, making it more accessible to an older crowd.

Bowie's musical style went through many reinventions. As a petulant artist, Bowie used acting as a new way to express himself and in turn, used the acting to bring new life to his music. Bowie of the '80s didn't have the legendary albums that he delivered in the '70s, but the one-two punch of "Modern Love" and "China Girl" on *Let's Dance* will stand alongside his best songs ever recorded.

Albums of the '80s:

Scary Monsters (And Super Creeps) (1980)
Let's Dance (1983)
Tonight (1984)
Never Let Me Down (1987)

The 11 Best Songs By David Bowie:

1. **Modern Love** (*Let's Dance*)
2. **China Girl** (*Let's Dance*)
3. **Neighborhood Threat** (*Tonight*)
4. **Bang Bang** (*Never Let Me Down*)
5. **Blue Jean** (*Tonight*)
6. **Criminal World** (*Let's Dance*)
7. **Scary Monsters and Super Creeps** (*Scary Monsters (And Super Creeps)*)
8. **Magic Dance** (*Labyrinth*)
9. **Because You're Young** (*Scary Monsters(And Super Creeps)*)
10. **Loving The Alien** (*Tonight*)
11. **Tumble and Twirl** (*Tonight*)

Fun Fact: Sting, Prince, Mick Jagger and Michael Jackson were all considered for the role of the Goblin King in Labyrinth before the producers decided on David Bowie. Bowie almost dropped out of the movie on two occasions because he felt the script didn't have enough humor in it.

KATE BUSH

I took drama in high school. After our final performance of *Meet Me in St. Louis*, we all went back to whoever's house didn't have parents in town for the night, where we had a wrap party. In the midst of a heated argument over whether *Robocop* was a cinematic masterpiece or a piece of trite, someone decided to put on Kate Bush's *Hounds of Love*. Right at the moment when I was defending that shooting somebody with 400 bullets did not constitute too much violence, Kate's sultry voice burst forward like lightning from a cloud. We all stopped arguing and just listened to the music. Maybe we were all really intoxicated, but Kate had us all mesmerized, pulling us into her world of sensual music. If an artist is so good that they can distract you from talking about *Robocop*, then there's something extraordinary about them.

Kate Bush may be a pop artist but there nothing poppy about her.   Kate's music was twisted.   There was something seriously wrong with her, in the best way possible. Diving into a Kate Bush album was like swimming through the murky waters of the Amazon while tripping on LSD. It was like flying without leaving the ground. If you stripped away all distractions and let one of Kate's albums envelop you, it left you feeling like you had a deeper understanding of life.

Most importantly, *Robocop* is still cinematic perfection.

Albums of the '80s:

Never For Ever (1980)
The Dreaming (1982)
Hounds of Love (1985)
The Sensual World (1989)

The 11 Best Songs By Kate Bush:

1. **Hounds of Love** (*Hounds of Love*)
2. **Running Up That Hill (A Deal With God)** (*Hounds of Love*)
3. **This Woman's Work** (*The Sensual World*)
4. **Cloudbusting** (*Hounds of Love*)
5. **The Big Sky** (*Hounds of Love*)
6. **Deeper Understanding** (*The Sensual World*)
7. **Burning Bridge** (*Cloudbusting single*)
8. **Suspended In Gaffa** (*The Dreaming*)
9. **And Dream of Sheep** (*Hounds of Love*)
10. **The Sensual World** (*The Sensual World*)
11. **The Wedding List** (*Never For Ever*)

Fun Fact: When she was 14, Kate Bush's family friend (Ricky Hopper), sent her demos to record labels. After a series of rejections, Hopper brought the demos to his old friend, David Gilmour. Gilmour's band, Pink Floyd, was fairly well known, and with his help, Kate was signed to a record label.

CAMEO

Despite funk being the least represented and least appreciated genre of the '80s, without funk there would be no backbone to many dance hits during the decade. Funk is all about the bass and it doesn't hurt if your sporting a hi-top fade haircut. Luckily, Larry Blackmon and his band Cameo had you covered. Finding their way out of the disco-crazed '70s, Cameo charged into the decade shaking our pants with songs that erupted with bass-pounding grooves that sent shivers up the Richter scale. Larry Blackmon was the 80s funk master. Blackmon's distinctive nasal croon toed the line between creepy lecherous uncle and a wild sex machine from the future. His signature "Ow!" beckoned listeners like the mating call of a tropical bird in heat. With a rhythm section that could hold their own with the best funk that Prince and the Revolution had to offer, Cameo was keeping dance floors hot. Cameo may be best known for their top ten smash hit, "Word Up!" and because of this song's success, they are commonly referred to as a one-hit wonder. Cameo was anything but a one-hit wonder. In fact, it was never about the hits for Cameo, it was all about the party. Many Cameo songs feature floor-thumping, eardrum popping bass solos that ravaged on for days at a time. These were not radio friendly numbers because they were not supposed to be. They were songs meant to be experienced live. Cameo made dance music with adrenaline that made you want to get up and get freaky. No party is complete without some freaks.

Albums of the '80s:

The Cameosis (1980)
Feel Me (1980)
Knights Of The Sound Table (1981)
Alligator Woman (1982)
Style (1983)
She's Strange (1984)
Single Life (1985)
Word Up! (1986)
Machismo (1988)

The 11 Best Songs By Cameo:

1. **Style** (*Style*)
2. **Freaky Dancin'** (*Knights Of The Sound Table*)
3. **Word Up!** (*Word Up!*)
4. **Candy** (*Word Up!*)
5. **Attack Me With Your Love** (*Single Life*)
6. **You Can Have The World** (*Word Up!*)
7. **Soul Army** (*Alligator Woman*)
8. **Throw It Down** (*Feel Me*)
9. **Be Yourself** (*Alligator Woman*)
10. **Aphrodisiac** (*Style*)
11. **Alligator Woman/Secrets of Time** (*Alligator Woman*)

Fun Fact: Bassist Aaron Mills, who played on a majority of Cameo's albums, would leave the band in the late '90s to join the hip-hop group, Outkast.

THE CARS

In the '80s, characters on screen were defined by their cars. *The Dukes of Hazzard* had the General Lee, *Magnum, P.I.* had his Ferrari, *The A-Team* had their black van, *The Fall Guy* (∞) had his GMC long bed truck, and Marty McFly had his time-traveling Delorean. The most memorable car of the decade had to be the Pontiac Firebird Trans Am from the iconic TV show, *Knight Rider*. What made *Knight Rider's* Trans Am unique, was that it could talk. K.I.T.T. (Knight Industries Two Thousand) was a futuristic crime-fighting robot that was also a freaking car! It was the coolest invention to anyone under the age of 12. The show also starred Germany-famous David Hasselhoff. Or, as he's better known: the Hoff. Of all the suave guys who solved crimes in the '80s, David Hasselhoff had to be the suaviest. He was an amalgam of all the other TV detectives. He had Tom Selleck's sexy and Lee Majors' grit. He drove like Crockett & Tubbs, and he was fearless like Bo & Luke. The Hoff was the man we all wanted to be, and he drove the car we all wanted.

The Cars were the coolest band of the '80s. With Ric Ocasek waltzing on stage in dark sunglasses and his lady killer voice, accompanied by Benjamin Orr's cool guy strut, you felt lucky that the band even bothered to share their time with you instead of flying private jets and partying with supermodels. They had an edge of mystery that enhanced the seduction. Are the Cars the David Hasselhoff of '80s rock bands? No, that would be impossible.

Albums of the '80s:

Panorama (1980)

Shake It Up (1981)

Heartbeat City (1984)

Door To Door (1987)

The 11 Best Songs By The Cars:

1. **You Might Think** (*Heartbeat City*)
2. **Tonight She Comes** (*Greatest Hits*)
3. **Heartbeat City** (*Heartbeat City*)
4. **Gimme Some Slack** (*Panorama*)
5. **Shake It Up** (*Shake It Up*)
6. **Magic** (*Heartbeat City*)
7. **Stranger Eyes** (*Heartbeat City*)
8. **Cruiser** (*Shake It Up*)
9. **Hello Again** (*Heartbeat City*)
10. **Drive** (*Heartbeat City*)
11. **Go Away** (*Door To Door*)

Fun Fact: The Cars video for their song "Hello Again" was directed by infamous pop art icon, Andy Warhol. The video was a statement on gratuitous sex and violence that was being overly exploited in music videos that were marketed to young kids.

(∞) **80s Note:** *The Fall Guy* was a TV show about a Hollywood stuntman who would solve crimes with the help of his giant truck.

THE CLASH

Punk rock arrived without warning. One minute the world was doing the Hustle, the next minute we were shaving our heads and beating the crap out of the guy next to us because we liked it. Punk was an exposé of poorly tuned guitars, savage drumming, and guttural screams that spoke to the pent-up anger, the rejection, and the disappointing realization that life wasn't as cheery as promised. Then, it was gone. As soon as punk's riotous fist struck the jaw of the establishment elite, many punk acts vanished into the ether. While plenty of new angry youths rose up out of the ashes to carry the torch of nihilism, one punk pioneer did blaze into the '80s. The Clash became the only band that mattered. While many punk acts screamed for political implosion, The Clash focused on social criticism. They didn't want destruction; they wanted change. They were the voice of the impoverished, the voice of the wrongly convicted, they were the voice of the disillusioned who just wanted to be heard. Like vagabond idealists preaching from a garage, The Clash broke down the door of social injustice like a preacher shouting his throat raw just to reach the parishioner in the back of the room. They threw everything against the wall because to spark a revolution, you have to have the endurance to see it through to the end. Their '80s album, *Sandinista!* was a triple album of music so influenced by international music that it had its own UN ambassador. As the last band of the first wave of punk, the Clash carried on for all the bands that couldn't be there with them.

Albums of the '80s:

London Calling (1980)

Sandinista! (1980)

Combat Rock (1982)

Cut The Crap (1985)

The 11 Best Songs By The Clash:

1. **London Calling** (*London Calling*)
2. **Police on My Back** (*Sandinista!*)
3. **Clampdown** (*London Calling*)
4. **This Is Radio Clash** (*This Is Radio Clash Single*)
5. **Know Your Rights** (*Combat Rock*)
6. **Rock The Casbah** (*Combat Rock*)
7. **Train In Vain** (*London Calling*)
8. **Straight To Hell** (*Combat Rock*)
9. **Should I Stay or Should I Go** (*Combat Rock*)
10. **Guns of Brixton** (*London Calling*)
11. **The Magnificent Seven** (*Sandinista!*)

Fun Fact: Joe Strummer was an avid runner and reportedly ran the Paris marathon and the London marathon. His best time to run the 26.2 miles was 4 hours and 13 minutes, which is less than ten minutes per mile.

Song Note (London Calling): The lyrics refer to all the different ways that the world could end including ice age, floods, starvation, and nuclear war.

THE COCTEAU TWINS

There is no other band that sounds like the Cocteau Twins. There was no band before them and there has been no band that has followed them. They are an anomaly. They are almost impossible to describe since there is no other artist to compare them to. Musically, they sound like an ethereal dream come to life. Close your eyes and imagine yourself walking through the wide open pastures of Scotland's landscape. Imagine the flora and all the colors. Now, turn off all the lights, let the light of the moon illuminate the field and replace all the bright colors with neon. That scratches the surface of the atmosphere that springs to life from the haunting, romantic melodies and graceful basslines. At other times, I imagine their gothic ballads were played at a Victorian ball for Romanian vampires in the 1880s. Their music transcends time. But the true reason that the band's esoteric nature is so distinct is because of the otherworldly vocals by lead singer Elizabeth Fraser. If angels could sing, they would consider themselves lucky if they sounded like Fraser. Her hypnotic voice is so light and airy, it feels like it has the power to float you up into the heavens. Fraser's magnetic voice lures you in with a piercing intensity that transports you to another dimension. Is she an enchantress? Is she a magical Elven princess? Is she a mermaid with siren-like powers? The Cocteau Twins are a glorious enigma, whose mystique is as alluring as it is mysterious.

Albums of the '80s:

Garlands (1982)
Head Over Heels (1983)
Treasure (1984)
Victorialand (1986)
The Moon And The Melodies (1986)
Blue Bell Knoll (1988)

The 11 Best Songs By The Cocteau Twins:

1. **Blue Bell Knoll** (*Blue Bell Knoll*)
2. **In Our Angelhood** (*Head Over Heels*)
3. **Musette and Drums** (*Head Over Heels*)
4. **Aloysius** (*Treasure*)
5. **Five Ten Fiftyfold** (*Head Over Heels*)
6. **Ivo** (*Treasure*)
7. **Those Eyes, That Mouth** (*Love's Easy Tears*)
8. **Wax and Wane** (*Garlands*)
9. **Pearly-'Dewdrops' Drops** (*The Spangle Maker*)
10. **Carolyn's Fingers** (*Blue Bell Knoll*)
11. **Pandora (For Cindy)** (*Treasure*)

Fun Fact: The band named themselves after the song "The Cocteau Twins" by Johnny and the Self-Abusers (who later changed their name to their more recognizable moniker, Simple Minds).

THE CULT

I bought the Cult's *Electric* album on cassette when I was in middle school. My mom was not stoked with my purchase questioning the content that I might be listening to with my easily influenced pre-teen mind. On the shelf next to it was Debbie Gibson's *Out of the Blue*, which historically speaking was a far more corruptive force, and my mom should have been happy that I had chosen my music so wisely. Gibson's sugary lab-coated fictional pop glaze had no redeeming nutritional value. Despite the sinister implied name, The Cult is a band that has far more creative substance than anyone gives them credit for. The Cult was an unbridled, aggressive force that infected your ears and coursed through your body like a leather-clad motorcycle gang plowing through a desert town, leaving nothing in their wake but a dismal trail of broken hearts and pruned hedges. Listening to the Cult was like sitting in an electric chair, rigged with a thousand volts of rock n' roll. The music made you feel more alive than a resurrected serial killer from a Wes Craven movie. Maybe the Cult couldn't dance as well as Ozone, Turbo or Debbie Gibson but that's because they didn't need to; the Cult made music that didn't need to overcompensate with pomp for lack of character. Their music had its own spirit animal that transformed our minds like an altered beast. As a teenager, their music gave me hope. Debbie Gibson may have sung the song "Electric Youth," but it's the Cult's *Electric* album that clearly spoke to America's youth.

Albums of the '80s:

Dreamtime (1984)
Love (1985)
Electric (1987)
Sonic Temple (1989)

The 11 Best Songs By The Cult:

1. **She Sells Sanctuary** (*Love*)
2. **Love Removal Machine** (*Electric*)
3. **Fire Woman** (*Sonic Temple*)
4. **Wild Flower** (*Electric*)
5. **83rd Dream** (*Dreamtime*)
6. **Sun King** (*Sonic Temple*)
7. **Soldier Blue** (*Sonic Temple*)
8. **Rain** (*Love*)
9. **Nirvana** (*Love*)
10. **Spiritwalker** (*Dreamtime*)
11. **Little Face** (*Rain*)

Fun Fact: Lead singer Ian Ashbury and guitarist Billy Duffy were founding members of the Hollywood United FC, an adult soccer team in Los Angeles. Other notable members included Paul Cook and Steve Jones of the Sex Pistols along with Vivian Campbell of Def Leppard.

Song Note (Wild Flower): The song is about Wolfchild, a character who over-indulges in sex, drugs and alcohol. Wolfchild is singer Ian Astbury's alter ego.

THE CURE

There's a belief among my cine-geek friends that Spielberg (possibly the greatest director of all time) was actually the second-best film director to John Carpenter in the '80s. It is a bold statement to make considering the cinematic arsenal in Spielberg's 80's canon, which includes three Indiana Jones movies, *E.T.*, *Poltergeist,* and my favorite Spielberg film, *Empire of the Sun*. Spielberg's films were spectacles. On the other hand, John Carpenter's films were grounded in the human condition, drawing on the prevalent fears of the era. Easily, the greatest horror film ever made, Carpenter's *The Thing* isn't just an examination of the human condition in a secluded environment, but a statement on the geopolitical fear of the lingering Russian threat. From the post-nuclear future of *Escape From New York* to the hidden aliens living among us in *They Live,* Carpenter knew how to prey on our societal fears in spine-chilling ways. If *Big Trouble in Little China* has anything to add, Carpenter also liked to have fun.

The Cure is music's John Carpenter. While many bands were concerned with crafting the perfect pop songs to reach chart-topping gold, The Cure created songs to embrace their audience on a deeply personal level. Their songs had a connective tissue that gave their listeners solace in their darkest moments. To the outside listener, The Cure may come across as moody and depressing, but if you listened to their lyrics, they weren't embracing the darkness but exposing the light in the times we needed it the most.

Albums of the '80s:

Seventeen Seconds (1980)
Faith (1981)
Pornography (1982)
The Top (1984)
The Head On The Door (1985)
Kiss Me, Kiss Me, Kiss Me (1987)
Disintegration (1989)

The 11 Best Songs By The Cure:

1. **Disintegration** (*Disintegration*)
2. **A Forest** (*Seventeen Seconds*)
3. **A Night Like This** (*Head on the Door*)
4. **Lovesong** (*Disintegration*)
5. **Primary** (*Faith*)
6. **Just Like Heaven** (*Kiss Me, Kiss Me, Kiss Me*)
7. **Prayers For Rain** (*Disintegration*)
8. **How Beautiful You Are** (*Kiss Me, Kiss Me, Kiss Me*)
9. **Pictures of You** (*Disintegration*)
10. **Push** (*Head on the Door*)
11. **Same Deep Water As You** (*Disintegration*)

Fun Fact: Lead singer Robert Smith claims to have recorded a solo album in 1983, which he plans to release when the Cure has officially broken up. We're still waiting.

THE dB'S

In the 1986 World Series, the Boston Red Sox led the New York Mets three games to two. In game six, Boston was ahead, when the Mets loaded the bases. A short dribbler off Mookie Wilson's bat rolled to first baseman, Bill Buckner. It should have been an easy out but the ball rolled through Buckner's legs! The Mets scored, won the game and went on to win the series. This wasn't the play that cost the Red Sox the series; there was still a game seven the Sox could have won. Even though a massive earthquake would hit San Francisco during the 1989 World Series (∞), killing dozens, to a Boston fan, Buckner's error was the worst thing that ever happened during a baseball game.

The dB's are one of the many '80s bands that fell short of breakout success. Though they're grouped in the same Southern genre as R.E.M., the band formed in New York and has as much post-punk, pub rock in them as they do any sort of jangle. The dB's were really two bands. Peter Holsapple and Christ Stamey are the lead vocalists and songwriters, who alternate duties from song to song. Their styles vary widely and can sound like two completely different bands. Right as the dB's were getting the attention of the big labels, Chris Stamey quit the band. Holsapple pushed forward, but there was always something missing. The dB's failed to get commercial traction and broke-up at the end of the decade. Would the dB's have won the World Series if Stamey didn't quit? Only Bill Buckner knows.

Albums of the '80s:

Stands For Decibels (1981)
Repercussion (1982)
Like This (1984)
The Sounds of Music (1987)

The 11 Best Songs By The dBs:

1. **Love Is For Lovers** (*Like This*)
2. **Amplifier** (*Repercussion*)
3. **Big Brown Eyes** (*Stands For Decibels*)
4. **Black and White** (*Stands For Decibels*)
5. **Neverland** (*Repercussion*)
6. **Happenstance** (*Repercussion*)
7. **Bad Reputation** (*Stands For Decibels*)
8. **Molly Says** (*The Sound of Music*)
9. **I Lie** (*The Sound of Music*)
10. **Tearjerkin'** (*Stands For Decibels*)
11. **The Fight** (*Stands For Decibels*)

Fun Fact: Before joining the dB's, Chris Stamey was in a band called Sneakers with Mitch Easter of Let's Active.

(∞) **80s Note:** In 1989, a 6.9 earthquake struck the Bay area of California during the first game of the World Series between the San Francisco Giants and the Oakland A's. The World Series was delayed while the cities recovered. Eventually, the World Series would resume and Oakland would win, sweeping thing Giants in four games.

DEAD KENNEDYS

Ronald Reagan was the US President for most of the '80s. Americans are split on whether he was the best President of modern times or he was the worst thing to happen to politics outside of Michael Dukakis. Those who praise Reagan accredit him for Reaganomics, appointing the first female supreme court justice, and ending the Cold War. Meanwhile, his detractors point out the Reaganvilles, a ballooning deficit, and the Iran Contra affair. Despite Reagan being a famous ex-actor, it was other celebrities that blasted him the most. The Dead Kennedys led the charge. The band's very first single in the late 1970s was called "California Über Alles," which was a public indictment of then-Governor of California, Jerry Brown. (Yep, the same Jerry Brown... weird, right?) With analogies to the German Third Reich, the band blasted the rise to power of the hippie movement that threatened us all. It was a mere few years later that another California governor, Reagan, became a target of their ire. In the updated version of the song, the band accused Reagan of favoring corporations over people, letting white supremacists influence the White House policies, invading Afghanistan, and starting World War III. While other musicians were more concerned with the eyes of classic Hollywood actresses, the Kennedys were keeping up the revolution while rallying against civil institutions. Ironically, since their break-up the band has spent much of their time in the civil institution of court, suing each other.

Albums of the '80s:

Fresh Fruit For Rotting Vegetables (1980)
Plastic Surgery Disasters (1982)
In God We Trust (1981)
Frankenchrist (1985)
Bedtime For Democracy (1986)
Give Me Convenience Or Give Me Death (1987)

The 11 Best Songs By Dead Kennedys:

1. **Holiday in Cambodia** (*Fresh Fruit For Rotting Vegetables*)
2. **Let's Lynch The Landlord** (*Fresh Fruit For Rotting Vegetables*)
3. **I Spy** (*Bedtime For Democracy*)
4. **Too Drunk To Fuck** (*Single*)
5. **Kill The Poor** (*Fresh Fruit For Rotting Vegetables*)
6. **Moon Over Marin** (*Plastic Surgery Disasters*)
7. **Chemical Warfare** (*Fresh Fruit For Rotting Vegetables*)
8. **Police Truck** (*Holiday in Cambodia*)
9. **This Could Be Anywhere (This Could Be Everywhere)** (*Frankenchrist*)
10. **Bleed For Me** (*Plastic Surgery Disasters*)
11. **Cesspools in Eden** (*Bedtime For Democracy*)

Fun Fact: Lead singer Jello Biafra ran for the mayor of San Francisco. Out of ten candidates, he came in fourth. After the election, a rule was passed that no one could run for mayor using a funny name.

Set Break/III Best Rap Songs of the Decade

Before hip-hop was dominated by production machines, samples and every aid known to songwriters of any genre, it started as nothing more than a rapper and a beat. It was raw, candid, and unrelenting. The '80s rap scene was a moment in time that will never be duplicated. These artists cared very little for radio play because none of them thought it was even possible. This is rap in its purest form and at its unbridled best.

Here are the 111 Best Rap Songs:

1. **King of Rock** - Run D.M.C. (*King of Rock*)
2. **Fight the Power** - Public Enemy (*Do The Right Thing Soundtrack*)
3. **Straight Outta Compton** - N.W.A. (*Straight Outta Compton*)
4. **Eric B. Is President** - Eric B. & Rakim (*Paid In Full*)
5. **The Message** - Grandmaster Flash & The Furious Five (*The Message*)
6. **You Gots To Chill** - EPMD (*Strictly Business*)
7. **Criminal Minded** - Boogie Down Productions (*Criminal Minded*)
8. **It Takes Two** - Rob Base & DJ E-Z Rock (*It Takes Two*)
9. **Paul Revere** - Beastie Boys (*License To Ill*)
10. **The Breaks** - Kurtis Blow (*Kurtis Blow*)
11. **Boyz-N-The Hood (remix)** - Eazy-E (*Eazy-Duz-It*)
12. **I'm Bad** - LL Cool J (*Bigger and Deffer*)
13. **Ain't No Half Steppin'** - Big Daddy Kane (*Long Live The Kane*)

14. **Rock Box** - Run D.M.C. (*Run D.M.C.*)
15. **That's The Joint** - Funky 4 + 1 (*That's The Joint*)
16. **White Lines (Don't Do It)** - Grandmaster Melle Mel (*White Lines*)
17. **Colors** - Ice-T (*Colors Soundtrack*)
18. **The New Rap Language** - Treacherous Three featuring Spoonie Gee (*Love Rap*)
19. **Microphone Fiend** - Eric B. & Rakim (*Follow The Leader*)
20. **La Di Da Di** - Doug E. Fresh featuring Slick Rick (*The Show/La Di Da Di*)
21. **Don't Believe The Hype** - Public Enemy (*It Takes A Nation of Millions To Hold Us Back*)
22. **My Philosophy** - Boogie Down Productions (*By All Means Necessary*)
23. **Children's Story** - Slick Rick (*The Great Adventures of Slick Rick*)
24. **Ladies First** - Queen Latifah featuring Monie Love (All Hail The Queen)
25. **Going Back To Cali** - LL Cool J (*Walking With A Panther*)
26. **Me Myself and I** - De La Soul (*3 Feet High and Rising*)
27. **Ego Trippin'** - Ultramagnetic MC's (*Critical Beatdown*)
28. **Five Minutes of Funk** - Whodini (*Escape*)
29. **Planet Rock** - Afrika Bambaataa (*Planet Rock: The Album*)
30. **Follow The Leader** - Eric B. & Rakim (*Follow The Leader*)
31. **I'm Your Pusher** - Ice-T (*Power*)
32. **Express Yourself** - N.W.A. (*Straight Outta Compton*)
33. **Fresh, Wild, Fly & Bold** - Cold Crush Brothers (*Fresh, Wild, Fly & Bold*)
34. **Brooklyn Queens** - 3rd Bass (*The Cactus Album*)
35. **Sucker M.C.'s** - Run D.M.C. (*Run D.M.C.*)

36. **Talkin' All That Jazz** - Stetsasonic (*In Full Gear*)
37. **No Sleep Til Brooklyn** - Beastie Boys (*License To Ill*)
38. **It's Tricky** - Run D.M.C. (*Raising Hell*)
39. **Set It Off** - Big Daddy Kane (*Long Live The Kane*)
40. **The Symphony** - Marley Marl (*In Control, Volume 1*)
41. **So Wat Cha Sayin'** - EPMD (*Unfinished Business*)
42. **South Bronx** - Boogie Down Productions (*Criminal Minded*)
43. **Cha Cha Cha** - MC Lyte (*Eyes On This*)
44. **Eazy-er Said Than Dunn** - Eazy-E (*Eazy-Duz-It*)
45. **P.S.K. What Does It Mean** - Schoolly D (*Schoolly D*)
46. **Roxanne Roxanne** - UTFO (*UTFO*)
47. **Top Billin'** - Audio Two (*What More Can I Say?*)
48. **Dog 'N The Wax** - Ice-T (*Rhyme Pays*)
49. **Jazzy Sensation (Bronx Version)** - Afrika Bambaataa and the Jazzy Five (*Jazzy Sensation*)
50. **It's My Thing** - EPMD (*Strictly Business*)
51. **The New Style** - Beastie Boys (*License To Ill*)
52. **It's Funky Enough** - The D.O.C. (*No One Can Do It Better*)
53. **Rebel Without A Pause** - Public Enemy (*It Takes A Nation of Millions To Hold Us Back*)
54. **I Know You Got Soul** - Eric B. & Rakim (*Paid In Full*)
55. **I Can't Live Without My Radio** - LL Cool J (*Radio*)
56. **Warm It Up Kane** - Big Daddy Kane (*It's A Big Daddy Thing*)
57. **Strong Island** - JVC Force (*Strong Island*)
58. **The Show** - Doug E. Fresh and the Get Fresh Crew (*The Show/La Di Da Di*)
59. **Step Off** - Grandmaster Melle Mel & Furious Five (*Step Off*)
60. **Make The Music With Your Mouth, Biz** - Biz Markie (*Make The Music With Your Mouth, Biz*)
61. **Say No Go** - De La Soul (*3 Feet High and Rising*)

62. **Weekend** - Cold Crush Brothers (*Weekend*)
63. **Go Stetsa** - Stetsasonic (*Go Stetsa*)
64. **The Bridge Is Over** - Boogie Down Productions (*Criminal Minded*)
65. **Fuck Tha Police** - N.W.A. (*Straight Outta Compton*)
66. **Shadrach** - Beastie Boys (*Paul's Boutique*)
67. **Bust A Move** - Young MC (*Stone Cold Rhymin'*)
68. **The Bridge** - MC Shan (*Down By Law*)
69. **Self Destruction** - Stop The Violence Movement (*Self Destruction*)
70. **Catch The Beat** - T-Ski Valley (*Catch The Beat*)
71. **Vapors** - Biz Markie (*Goin' Off*)
72. **Road To The Riches** - Kool G Rap & DJ Polo (*Road To The Riches*)
73. **B-Boy Bouillabaisse** - Beastie Boys (*Paul's Boutique*)
74. **Rock The Bells** - LL Cool J (*Radio*)
75. **Hey Young World** - Slick Rick (*The Great Adventures of Slick Rick*)
76. **6 'n The Mornin'** - Ice T (*Rhyme Pays*)
77. **New York New York** - Grandmaster Flash & The Furious Five (*Greatest Messages*)
78. **Leader of the Pack** - UTFO (*UTFO*)
79. **Smooth Operator** - Big Daddy Kane (*It's A Big Daddy Thing*)
80. **Shake Your Rump** - Beastie Boys (*Paul's Boutique*)
81. **Just A Friend** - Biz Markie (*The Biz Never Sleeps*)
82. **The Formula** - The D.O.C. (*No One Can Do It Better*)
83. **I Ain't No Joke** - Eric B. & Rakim (*Paid In Full*)
84. **Watch Me Now** - Ultramagnetic MCs (*Critical Beatdown*)
85. **It's Like That** - Run D.M.C. (*Run D.M.C.*)
86. **Freaks Come Out At Night** - Whodini (*Escape*)
87. **My Part of Town** - Tuff Crew (*Back To Wreck Shop*)
88. **Rockin' It** - Fearless Four (*Rockin' It*)

89. **Black Steel in the Hour of Chaos** - Public Enemy (*It Takes A Nation of Millions To Hold Us Back*)
90. **Buddy** - De La Soul (*3 Feet High and Rising*)
91. **Go See The Doctor** - Kool Moe Dee (*Kool Moe Dee*)
92. **Making Cash Money** - Busy Bee Starski (*Making Cash Money*)
93. **Bite This** - Roxanne Shanté (*Bite This*)
94. **Feel the Heartbeat** - The Treacherous Three (*The Treacherous Three*)
95. **It's Yours** - T La Rock and Jazzy Jay (*It's Yours*)
96. **Night of the Living Baseheads** - Public Enemy (*It Takes A Nation of Millions To Hold Us Back*)
97. **The Body Rock** - The Treacherous Three (*The Treacherous Three*)
98. **Funky Cold Medina** - Tone Lōc (*Lōc -ed After Dark*)
99. **Peter Piper** - Run D.M.C. (*Raising Hell*)
100. **Paid In Full** - Eric B. & Rakim (*Paid In Full*)
101. **Brand New Funk** - DJ Jazzy Jeff and the Fresh Prince (*He's The DJ, I'm the Rapper*)
102. **Raw** - Big Daddy Kane (*Long Live The Kane*)
103. **The Gas Face** - 3rd Bass (*The Cactus Album*)
104. **Paper Thin** - MC Lyte (*Lyte As A Rock*)
105. **Manifest** - Gang Starr (*No More Mr. Nice Guy*)
106. **I Got It Made** - Special Ed (*Youngest In Charge*)
107. **Doowatchyalike** - Digital Underground (*Sex Packets*)
108. **My Melody** - Eric B. & Rakim (*Paid In Full*)
109. **Roxanne's Revenge** - Roxanne Shanté (*Roxanne's Revenge*)
110. **Do It Like A G.O.** - Geto Boys (*Grip It! On That Other Level*)
111. **(You Gotta) Fight For Your Right (To Party)** - Beastie Boys (*License To Ill*)

DEF LEPPARD

The space shuttle was one of the biggest stories of the decade. For unfortunate reasons, the biggest shuttle story was the biggest space tragedy. In 1986, the Challenger Space Shuttle exploded on launch, killing everyone aboard. I'll never forget how I found out. I was in art class when my teacher walked in with the least compassionate response ever and said, "The first teacher in space is the last teacher in space." I don't know what bothered me more, the tragic news or the apathetic delivery of the news by my teacher. To my *Star Wars* loving brain, the space shuttle represented the final frontier. To find out that it was mortal, it ended a piece of my childhood. But the shuttle program persevered and proved that in the 80s, we had resilience.

Def Leppard was the band that taught me that rock stars were mortal, too. In 1984, drummer Rick Allen lost his arm in a car accident. For a drummer to lose his arm, it's a fate worse than death. At least in death, you're immortalized. In dismemberment, Allen was rendered all but obsolete. But he didn't give up. Allen didn't whine about it or complain about it. He found a way to fix the problem and drummed on. He created new types of foot pedals so he could compensate by drumming with his feet. It worked. Allen's drumming didn't miss a beat. The band's next album became its biggest success, selling over 10 million copies. Def Leppard defined resilience and grew stronger because of it. Are you getting it... really getting it? They did.

Albums of the '80s:

High 'N' Dry (1980)
On Through The Night (1981)
Pyromania (1983)
Hysteria (1987)

The 11 Best Songs By Def Leppard:

1. **Photograph** (*Pyromania*)
2. **It Don't Matter** (*On Through The Night*)
3. **Satellite** (*On Through The Night*)
4. **Lady Strange** (*High 'N' Dry*)
5. **Wasted** (*On Through The Night*)
6. **You Got Me Runnin'** (*High 'N' Dry*)
7. **Animal** (*Hysteria*)
8. **Rock Brigade** (*On Through The Night*)
9. **Love Bites** (*Hysteria*)
10. **Mirror Mirror (Look Into My Eyes)** (*High 'N' Dry*)
11. **Too Late For Love** (*Pyromania*)

Fun Fact: Their album, *Pyromania*, was a huge success in America, selling 7 million copies. But in their home country of England, they were slightly less successful, selling only 60,000 copies.

Song Note (Animal): After four albums, this was the first song that was a hit for Def Leppard in their home country of the U.K.

DEPECHE MODE

On June 18, 1988, Depeche Mode did the impossible. They sold out the Rose Bowl. This was a band that received very little airplay outside of modern rock radio stations. They were widely perceived as a "niche" band. Many critics said they would be shocked if the band managed to sell out 20,000 tickets on the floor. Depeche Mode went on to sell over 65,000 tickets which were a few thousand more than the reunited Eagles would sell in the '90s. Depeche Mode had legitimized themselves as a band that deserved respect.

Haters of the band called them whiny, boring, depressing... Depeche Mope. Depeche Mode isn't depressing, Depeche Mode is life. Underneath the dark, sultry bass lines, brooding with emotion is a band who is brimming with love, hope, and spirituality. Their songs bare all, exposing their weaknesses to the world in search of making that connection with their fans. Fanatics, really. Depeche Mode is a connective tissue that spreads across a global fan base. Depeche Mode fans aren't just fans; they're family. The band's career isn't without its ups and down. I can't even remember how many times they've broken up and then reunited. Every time this happens, their fans stick with them, never giving up, like a golfer who doesn't give up on his perfect game of golf even in a lightning storm. That's what the greats do. They take time out to re-invent themselves to take their fans new plateaus. Depeche Mode isn't just a band; they're a lifestyle.

Albums of the '80s:

Speak and Spell (1981)
A Broken Frame (1982)
Construction Time Again (1983)
Some Great Reward (1984)
Black Celebration (1986)
Music For the Masses (1987)

The 11 Best Songs By Depeche Mode:

1. **But Not Tonight** (*Black Celebration*)
2. **Never Let Me Down** (*Music For The Masses*)
3. **Photographic** (*Speak and Spell*)
4. **Everything Counts** (*Construction Time Again*)
5. **Blasphemous Rumors** (*Some Great Reward*)
6. **Strangelove** (*Music For The Masses*)
7. **Somebody** (*Some Great Reward*)
8. **Stripped** (*Black Celebration*)
9. **Lie To Me** (*Some Great Reward*)
10. **Shake The Disease** (*Catching Up With Depeche Mode*)
11. **Sacred** (*Music For The Masses*)

Fun Fact: Depeche Mode's "Concert for the Masses" that took place at the Rose Bowl, would be released as a concert album, called *101*. The title refers to the show being the 101st concert for the *Music For the Masses* Tour. The live album would be the band's second best-selling album of the '80s, only beat out by its parent album, *Music For The Masses*.

DEVO

On January 22nd, 1984, everyone in America was huddled around their television sets for Super Bowl XVIII to watch the Los Angeles Raiders (∞) obliterate the Washington Redskins by a score of 2,048,504 to 3. In this blow-out game, it wasn't the final score that was memorable. The touchstone moment was the commercial for Apple's new personal computer, the Macintosh. In this Orwellian-themed ad, Apple claimed that big brother (in reference to IBM) wouldn't take over the world because the Macintosh (an affordable personal computer) was here to save the day. And by affordable, I mean, $2,500. This was a huge commercial. It even had its own promotional campaign leading up to its release. The commercial had a profound impact on the world at large. It wasn't just the commercial's message that was important but what it represented: the era of the computer had arrived.

The new wave band, Devo, was obsessed with how our culture had become reliant on computer technology. The name of the band is in reference to the "D-evolution" of humankind. A humankind that stops thinking for itself and allows others (or machines) to do it for them. Devo's blistering, mechanical melodies and satirical lyrics were a social commentary on the herd-like mentality of our culture. They may have covered it up under sci-fi themes and surreal humor, but the cheeky delivery urged us to never abandon humanity.

Albums of the '80s:

Freedom of Choice (1980)
New Traditionalists (1981)
Oh, No! It's Devo (1982)
Shout (1984)
E-Z Listening (1987)
Total Devo (1988)
Baby Doll EP (1988)
Disco Dancer EP (1988)

The 11 Best Songs By Devo:

1. **Freedom of Choice** (*Freedom of Choice*)
2. **Girl U Want** (*Freedom of Choice*)
3. **Whip It** (*Freedom of Choice*)
4. **Patterns** (*Oh, No! It's Devo*)
5. **Gates of Steel** (*Freedom of Choice*)
6. **Turn Around** (*Whip It*)
7. **That's Good** (*Oh, No! It's Devo*)
8. **Jerkin' Back 'n' Forth** (*New Traditionalists*)
9. **Plain Truth** (*Total Devo*)
10. **Beautiful World** (*New Traditionalists*)
11. **I Wouldn't Do That To You** (*Happy Hour Soundtrack*)

Fun Fact: As expensive as it was, the Orwellian-themed commercial for Apple's Macintosh was only played once nationally.

(∞) **80s Note:** The Los Angeles Raiders were an NFL football team from 1982-1994 until they moved to Oakland.

DEHYS MIDNIGHT RUNNERS

Video arcades in the '80s were like the coffee shops of the '90s, except instead of caffeine, they peddled video games. The sole purpose of these video games was to beat the high score. If by chance you managed to get a top score on one of the games, you were given the most prestigious award possible: you were granted the privilege to put your initials in the game next to your score. Having the high score on Pac-Man in a local 7-11 was the closest thing we had to going viral. It wasn't easy. First, you had to wait in line to play, and there was always a really good teenager in front of you. Pac-Man had the longest wait because everyone loved the three intermissions that occurred in-between levels. I was never good enough to reach the third intermission, so I would sneak behind any skilled Pac-Fanatic to glimpse the elusive final act. Even though, it was a 20-second 8-bit animation of a ghost without a sheet; to my elementary school self, it was the Ark of the Covenant.

Dexys Midnight Runners was named after the drug Dexedrine, which like Pac-Man's power pellets, gave the user an explosive burst of energy. But Dexedrine users didn't utilize the energy to eat ghosts; they used it to dance all night. Because of this, the users were called "midnight runners," which is how the band got its name. Dexy's music was the ultimate power pellet. Their quick-paced, upbeat sound motivated every midnight runner to get up and dance in a blink (or a Clyde).

Albums of the '80s:

Searching For The Young Soul Rebels (1980)
Too-Rye-Ay (1982)
Don't Stand Me Down (1985)

The 11 Best Songs By Dexys Midnight Runners:

1. **Come On Eileen** (*Too-Rye-Ay*)
2. **Let's Make This Precious** (*Too-Rye-Ay*)
3. **Breakin' Down The Walls of Heartache** (*Geno*)
4. **Show Me** (*Show Me Single*)
5. **I Love You (Listen To This)** (*Don't Stand Me Down*)
6. **Jackie Wilson Said** (*I'm In Heaven When You Smile*) (*Too-Rye-Ay*)
7. **Burn It Down** (*Searching For The Young Soul Rebels*)
8. **Tell Me When My Light Turns Green** (*Searching For The Young Soul Rebels*)
9. **Seven Days Too Long** (*Searching For The Young Soul Rebels*)
10. **The Celtic Soul Brothers** (*Too-Rye-Ay*)
11. **There There My Dear** (*Searching For The Young Soul Rebels*)

Fun Fact: Despite the success of their debut album, *Searching For The Young Soul Rebels*, seven of the nine band members quit within a year of the album's release. Only singer, Kevin Rowland, and trombonist, "Big" Jim Paterson remained to re-form the band and start over.

DIO

I remember when Eddie Murphy's movie, *Raw*, came out. There was a line of people wrapped around the block, waiting to see it. Even though it was just Eddie Murphy doing stand-up, it was Eddie Murphy doing stand-up! We didn't have celebrities in the '80s; we had megastars. We had stars so big; it didn't matter what their movie was about, we just wanted to see them in it. Arnold Schwarzenegger is a robot from the future? I'm in. Sylvester Stallone takes on the entire Vietnam army? Buy me a ticket. Bruce Willis battles terrorists in an LA skyscraper? Sign me up. Our heroes didn't need capes. They were average men in impossible situations, who used their wits and charisma to defy the odds. Whether it was Jean-Claude Van Damme's accent, Eddie Murphy's laugh, or Robert DeNiro's mole, we were in line, ready to be entertained.

In the metal world, no other solo artist invoked a more powerful stigma than Ronnie James Dio. How great is Dio? He replaced the legendary Ozzy Osbourne as the singer of Black Sabbath and made one of the best-reviewed and highest-selling albums of Sabbath's career. And his solo career? His debut album, *Holy Diver*, is a cacophony of dimensions, the underlying lies behind every truth, the evil in everything that's good, a critical dissection of the dishonesty in romance and religion. It is considered to be one of the greatest metal albums ever made. That's not bad for a guy with only three letters in his name.

Albums of the '80s:

Holy Diver (1983)
The Last In Line (1984)
Sacred Heart (1985)
The Dio E.P. (1986)
Dream Evil (1987)

The 11 Best Songs By Dio:

1. **Holy Diver** (*Holy Diver*)
2. **Rainbow In The Dark** (*Holy Diver*)
3. **Evil Eyes** (*The Last In Line*)
4. **We Rock** (*The Last In Line*)
5. **Caught In The Middle** (*Holy Diver*)
6. **The Last In Line** (*The Last In Line*)
7. **King Of Rock and Roll** (*Sacred Heart*)
8. **Dream Evil** (*Dream Evil*)
9. **Stand Up and Shout** (*Holy Diver*)
10. **Faces In The Window** (*Dream Evil*)
11. **Hide In The Rainbow** (*The Dio E.P.*)

Fun Fact: In the late '80s, a Japanese video game company made a video game called *Holy Diver*, based on the Dio album and song of the same name. In this Castlevania-style game, the main character, who looked very similar to Ronnie James Dio, traveled through castles and levels to defeat demons. Probably the greatest tragedy of the '80s was that this game was only released in Japan but not the U.S.

THE DREAM SYNDICATE

Keeping track of musical genres in the '80s was like trying to decode the interweaving trails of Tron's light cycles. Metal was banging hair, rap was busting rhymes, pop was beatin' it and punk was screaming at walls. Even though it had only been ten years since it was the dominant genre in the late '60s, psychedelic rock had all but vanished. The Dream Syndicate formed to fill that void of raucous, rebellious rock. The Dream Syndicate was part of the Paisley Underground, a movement that featured bands who drew inspiration from the groovy tunes of the Mamas and Papas and the counter-culture of the Velvet Underground. The mainstream largely ignored the genre. Only The Bangles saw the hazy shade of pop radio significance due to the help from the genre's biggest fan: his purple majesty... Prince. Yes, that Prince. He loved the bands of the Paisley Underground so much, he named his label Paisley Park. (No, seriously.) While fellow Paisley artists like The Bangles and The Three O'Clock were having songs written by Prince, The Dream Syndicate emerged as the genre's king. Led by Steve Wynn's raspy, throaty grumble, the Dream Syndicate were the ultimate college party band. Not the one on the main floor doing covers; the band in the basement thrashing through improv jams, sweat spraying off their lips, screaming until their throats dried up from exhaustion. The Dream Syndicate's success stems from their collegiate spirit that if you rage hard enough, you can change the world. They didn't change the world but they played as if they could.

Albums of the '80s:

The Dream Syndicate EP (1982)
The Days of Wine and Roses (1982)
Medicine Show (1984)
Out of the Grey (1986)
Ghost Stories (1988)

The 11 Best Songs By The Dream Syndicate:

1. **The Days of Wine and Roses** (*The Days of Wine and Roses*)
2. **Forest For The Trees** (*Out of the Grey*)
3. **Then She Remembers** (*The Days of Wine and Roses*)
4. **Definitely Clean** (*The Days of Wine and Roses*)
5. **Burn** (*Medicine Show*)
6. **That's What You Always Say** (*The Days of Wine and Roses*)
7. **John Coltrane Stereo Blues** (*Medicine Show*)
8. **Loving The Sinner, Hating The Sin** (*Ghost Stories*)
9. **See That My Grave Is Kept Clean** (*Ghost Stories*)
10. **Bullet With My Name On It** (*Medicine Show*)
11. **Tell Me When It's Over** (*The Days of Wine and Roses*)

Fun Fact: Lead Singer Steve Wynn used to work at the Rhino Record store while studying at UCLA. Two of the regular customers were Susanna Hoffs and Vicki Peterson of the Bangles. They became fast friends.

DURAN DURAN

James Bond movies always had corny elements to them. In the '60s and '70s, the corny moments were more like cool ranch seasoning than the actual chip. In the '80s, the corniness became the chip. From being attacked by men in ice hockey gear to using traveling circuses to cover up for nuclear bombs, Bond movies began reflecting the oddball nature of the decade. Probably the corniest of all the Bond movies would have to be 1985's *A View To A Kill*. In the very opening scene, Roger Moore's James Bond created a make-shift snowboard to escape from rifle-toting Russians, while the Beach Boys "California Girls" played in the background. Watching that scene, there is no doubt that this was a movie that shouldn't be taken seriously. With Grace Jones as a menacing villain, there's little substance to separate it from an '80s sitcom. As a kid, I thought it was the best movie ever made, as an adult, not so much. The movie has one redeeming quality: Duran Duran's theme song "A View To A Kill." It is not only one of the best James Bond songs; it's one of Duran Duran's best overall. With pastel cotton suits, an unshaven lead singer, and the Doublemint-inspired band name, Duran Duran's flamboyant charisma was as seductive as it was charming. Strutting with fashionable sexiness, the band dominated MTV in the era when looks mattered most. With fluid sex appeal and R-rated videos, they became the perfect complement to the smooth swagger of Bond's tuxedos and martinis, dishing out a theme song that left the film shaken but not stirred.

Albums of the '80s:

Duran Duran (1980)
Rio (1982)
Seven and the Ragged Tiger (1983)
Decade (1989)

The 11 Best Songs By Duran Duran:

1. **Rio** (*Rio*)
2. **Save A Prayer** (*Rio*)
3. **Hungry Like The Wolf** (*Rio*)
4. **Union of the Snake** (*Seven and the Ragged Tiger*)
5. **A View To A Kill** (*Decade*)
6. **New Moon On Monday** (*Seven and the Ragged Tiger*)
7. **Girls on Film** (*Duran Duran*)
8. **Shadows on Your Side** (*Seven and the Ragged Tiger*)
9. **Anyone Out There** (*Duran Duran*)
10. **The Reflex** (*Seven and the Ragged Tiger*)
11. **Is There Something I Should Know** (*Duran Duran*)

Fun Fact: Though bassist John Taylor, guitarist Andy Taylor and drummer Roger Taylor all have the same last name, despite rumors, none of them are related.

Song Note (Rio): Keyboardist Nick Rhodes created the song's opening chimes by throwing metal rods onto the strings of a grand piano, then playing the sound effect in reverse.

BOB DYLAN

Bob Dylan is a legend, an icon, an inspiration and a trailblazer. He has defined rock and roll, and he has spit in its face. He has legions of countless fans who sing his praises better than he can carry a tune. In no era has he pissed off more of his fans than in the '80s. This was the period when rebel rouser Dylan did the unthinkable and roused the rebels themselves. In the late '70s, Dylan embraced establishment religion and became a born-again Christian. The man who wrote the words that would be battle cries for the '60s revolution had seemingly turned his back on his faithful followers. But Dylan's '80s period wasn't just a rebirth of his religious views; it was a tumultuously painful musical rebirth that would eventually lead to his introspective '90s emergence. Though Dylan had been groundbreaking all throughout his career, it was in the 80s where he was at his most confused, chaotic and experimental. He went from the religious-themed album, *Saved,* to a chorus singer on "We Are The World" to being a guest rapper on a Boogie Down Productions album. That's right... guest rapper. Believe it or not, Bob Dylan may be one of the first guest rappers on a hip-hop album. Dylan stumbled through decade dipping his colloquial guitar in many areas, but it was at the end of the decade that Dylan fans jumped back into the fold when he joined the supergroup, The Traveling Wilburys. As we entered the '90s, Dylan was cool again. Or maybe he was always cool, and we were the ones who were not down in our groove.

Albums of the '80s:

Saved (1980)

Shot of Love (1981)

Infidels (1983)

Empire Burlesque (1985)

Knocked Out Loaded (1986)

Down In The Groove (1988)

Oh Mercy (1989)

The 11 Best Songs By Bob Dylan:

1. **Most of the Time** (*Oh Mercy*)
2. **Jokerman** (*Infidels*)
3. **Political World** (*Oh Mercy*)
4. **When The Night Comes Falling From The Sky** (*Empire Burlesque*)
5. **Brownsville Girl** (*Knocked Out Loaded*)
6. **I'll Remember You** (*Empire Burlesque*)
7. **Covenant Woman** (*Saved*)
8. **Sweetheart Like You** (*Infidels*)
9. **Emotionally Yours** (*Empire Burlesque*)
10. **Everything Is Broken** (*Oh Mercy*)
11. **Death Is Not The End** (*Down In the Groove*)

Fun Fact: In 1980, Bob Dylan finally won his first solo Grammy for the song "Gotta Serve Somebody."

Song Note (Brownsville Girl): Co-written by playwright, Sam Shepard, Dylan has only performed this song live once.

ECHO & THE BUNNYMEN

I truly believe that my eating habits were tarnished by '80s films. When I saw human eyeballs float to the top of the soup of the day in *Indiana Jones and the Temple of Doom*, I almost threw-up. I had an incredible fear of buffets after watching the man eat until he exploded in *Monty Python's Meaning of Life*. But the most Bulimic-inducing moment was in *The Lost Boys*. In one scene, a vampire biker gang (led by Kiefer Sutherland) is eating take-out Chinese food. One of the vampires was eating steamed rice, only to look down and see that he was eating a container of maggots. After that, I didn't eat rice until the '90s. There was another haunting piece of that movie that has stuck with me all these years. It is the macabre version of The Doors song, "People Are Strange" by Echo & Bunnymen.

The Doors are the closest thing the '60s had to an alternative rock band. For Echo & the Bunnymen to increase the gloomy atmosphere of the song to make it vampire worthy, is quite the admirable achievement. But this wasn't a one-time success. Though Echo & The Bunnymen had the vampire party music staked out, the rest of their music conveyed a strong sense of hope. They had songs that were enriched with the concepts of heaven and hell, love and hate, porcupines and crocodiles. Their music was a celebration of the promises of life. They may have sounded like obsessive Giallo film fans, but in their lyrics, they embraced the sweet sugary ballyhoo of existence.

Albums of the '80s:

Crocodiles (1980)
Heaven Up Here (1981)
Porcupine (1983)
Ocean Rain (1984)
Echo & the Bunnymen (1987)

The 11 Best Songs By Echo & The Bunnymen:

1. **Bring on the Dancing Horses** (*Songs to Learn And Sing*)
2. **The Killing Moon** (*Ocean Rain*)
3. **Lips Like Sugar** (*Echo & the Bunnymen*)
4. **Rescue** (*Crocodiles*)
5. **Seven Seas** (*Ocean Rain*)
6. **Silver** (*Ocean Rain*)
7. **The Back of Love** (*Porcupine*)
8. **With A Hip** (*Heaven Up Here*)
9. **Bedbugs and Ballyhoo** (*Echo & the Bunnymen*)
10. **People Are Strange** (*Lost Boys Soundtrack*)
11. **Never Stop** (*Never Stop* single)

Fun Fact: Ian McCulloch, lead singer, is a huge soccer (football) fan. He is a season ticket holder for Liverpool FC. In 2006, when Liverpool won the FA Cup, McCulloch recorded an anthem for the event.

THE ENGLISH BEAT

Before Charlie Sheen became an A-list star in 1986's *Platoon*, he was known for making scene-stealing cameos, most notably in 1985's *Ferris Bueller's Day Off*. As a detained drug dealer, Charlie's character delivered the most poignant message of the movie to Ferris' sister, Jeanie. That message was to worry less about what others are doing and concentrate more on enjoying your own life. As we all know now, Charlie has lived his "real" life with that motto in mind. This theme runs rampant like a barrel-tossing ape through the whole decade. At its core, the '80s were about mindless fun. It was about cutting loose and enjoying life. That's why *Ferris Bueller's* end action sequence leaves such a lasting impact. In the scene, Ferris makes a mad dash through the backyards of his neighborhood racing his parents home. It's a footloose sprawl, sprinkled with the carefree spirit of letting go. That spirit embodies the music of The English Beat. "The Beat" (as they were referred to in the UK since everyone already knew they were English) created their own wild world. They transported their listeners to an island paradise where you could dance the night away with a beautiful woman or a chiseled man. Where the sun is always setting, and all the drinks come in coconut shells. The fanciful ambience of their music enhanced that final scene. It was no longer just a race to see who could win; it was about the joy of the race. It wasn't about who won; it was about having an unencumbered moment of pure bliss. A moment that any member of the general public could relate to.

Albums of the '80s:

I Just Can't Stop It (1980)
Wha'ppen? (1981)
Special Beat Service (1982)

The 11 Best Songs By The English Beat:

1. **Save It For Later** (*Special Beat Service*)
2. **Mirror in the Bathroom** (*I Just Can't Stop It*)
3. **Twist & Crawl** (*I Just Can't Stop It*)
4. **Too Nice To Talk To** (*Wha'ppen?*)
5. **Best Friend** (*I Just Can't Stop It*)
6. **I Confess** (*Special Beat Service*)
7. **Tears of A Clown** (*Single*)
8. **Sole Salvation** (*Special Beat Service*)
9. **Two Swords** (*I Just Can't Stop It*)
10. **Rotating Head** (*Special Beat Service*)
11. **Ranking Full Stop** (*Tears of a Clown Single*)

Fun Fact: For one of the band's first gigs, the members put up posters all over town promoting their show. The posters depicted a calendar girl holding a whip. The headlining act (a female-led band) thought the poster was sexist and went around town and tore them all down. After the show, the two bands ended up bonding with each other and later toured together.

THE FALL

Eighties kids were collectors. When we learned that our grandparents threw out all of our parents' baseball cards that were now worth thousands of dollars, we held on to everything. As baseball cards exploded in popularity, other sports joined them. We had football, baseball, hockey, and even NASCAR. Then movies got in on the action, creating collector cards for every type of media released. It was one thing to have *Star Wars* or *Star Trek* trading cards but did we really need cards for *Adventures in Babysitting*? *Young Guns 2*? *Three's Company*? *Alf*? Seriously...*Alf*! Collecting cards imploded when the Garbage Pail Kids cards were released. These were gross satirical renditions of Cabbage Patch Kids... and the grosser, the better. Crater Chris was a kid who was covered with oozing zits. We thought this was as low as it could go but then they made a *Garbage Pail Kids* movie and there was no coming back from that.

Being a fan of the Fall's avant-garde, jam-like scrappy, punk rock turned you into a collector, too. In the '80s, The Fall released nine studio albums, six live albums, four compilations, five EPs and 21 singles with B-sides, totaling over 200 songs. Collecting all their releases became a full-time activity, especially since they were an indie rock band with limited exposure. But the Fall's punch-in-the-gut passion, Mark E. Smith's drunken authoritarian voice, and their boundary-challenging melodies, they were a band worth the effort.

Albums of the '80s:

Grotesque (After The Gramme) (1980)
Hex Enduction Hour (1982)
Room To Live (1982)
Perverted By Language (1983)
The Wonderful and Frightening World Of... (1984)
This Nation's Saving Grace (1985)
Bend Sinister (1986)
The Frenz Experiment (1988)
I Am Kurious Oranj (1988)

The 11 Best Songs By The Fall:

1. **Cruiser's Creek** (*This Nation's Saving Grace*)
2. **Totally Wired** (*Totally Wired Single*)
3. **Victoria** (*The Frenz Experiment*)
4. **The Classical** (*Hex Enduction Hour*)
5. **The Container Drivers** (*Grotesque (After The Gramme)*)
6. **Jawbone and the Air Rifle** (*Hex Enduction Hour*)
7. **There's A Ghost In My House** (*The Frenz Experiment*)
8. **New Big Prinz** (*I Am Kurious Oranj*)
9. **Bombast** (*This Nation's Saving Grace*)
10. **Kicker Conspiracy** (*Perverted By Language*)
11. **L.A.** (*This Nation's Saving Grace*)

Fun Fact: In its 40-year existence, The Fall has had over 66 different members in the band. Up until his death, singer, Mark E. Smith, was the only member to be in the band for its entire career.

FOREIGNER

Growing up, I always thought Foreigner had the most gut-wrenching ballads. I was fascinated by how a band could wallow in such heartache. Aren't they rock stars? Don't they have women throwing themselves at their feet? What do they have to be sad about? If a girl breaks up with them, can't they just go into the next room and pick out a new one? At least that's what my ten-year-old mind fathomed. Because every time I heard one of Foreigner's ballads, I felt compelled to cry about the women who had left me. And I had never had a girlfriend. What did I know?

Foreigner was a '70s rock force that found themselves in the synth-heavy '80s, needing to reinvent their guitar-driven sound. While most of the '70s bands floundered, only a few managed to re-imagine their dreams and find a new sound that complemented their former selves. Foreigner did it with such dominance; it made a lot of people forget that they were even a '70s band to begin with. While they only had three albums out in the '80s, the band found their biggest commercial success in the decade. The timing was right, as if they had been revving their engines until they finally hit 88 mph. It takes talent to have one radio hit, but it takes a special proclivity to evolve and succeed in multiple decades. Instead of waiting to know what it takes to make a jukebox hero, as foreigners, the band figured out how to survive wherever they landed.

Albums of the '80s:

4 (1981)
Agent Provocateur (1984)
Inside Information (1987)

The 11 Best Songs By Foreigner:

1. **Juke Box Hero** (*4*)
2. **I Want To Know What Love Is** (*Agent Provocateur*)
3. **That Was Yesterday** (*Agent Provocateur*)
4. **Say You Will** (*Inside Information*)
5. **Urgent** (*4*)
6. **Face to Face** (*Inside Information*)
7. **Heart Turns To Stone** (*Inside Information*)
8. **Waiting On A Girl Like You** (*4*)
9. **A Love In Vain** (*Agent Provocateur*)
10. **Luanne** (*4*)
11. **Girl On The Moon** (*4*)

Fun Fact: The band was originally named Trigger but changed it because another band had that name. They chose Foreigner because the band members were British and American and would therefore always be foreigners in any country they traveled to.

Song Note (Urgent): The signature synth sound comes from keyboardist, Thomas Dolby, who would go on to have a big solo hit with "She Blinded Me With Science."

PETER GABRIEL

Many iconic songs from the '80s owe their legendary status to the music video. The emergence of MTV as a guiding force in what song was cool played a major role in marrying songs to their videos. You cannot remember Michael Jackson's "Thriller" without a flashback to a gang of breakdancing zombies. You cannot remember Tom Petty's "Don't Come Around Here No More" without recalling the Mad Hatter. And, you cannot remember Peter Gabriel's "Sledgehammer" without conjuring up the nightmarish stop-motion animation of the video. Despite "Sledgehammer" being one of the most groundbreaking videos of the decade, it is by no means the most iconic image tied to a Peter Gabriel song. It wasn't just MTV that immortalized songs with a visual image; movies provided an incredible outlet for artists to spread their music to the masses. Peter Gabriel's "In Your Eyes" may be the most distinct of them all. In all of '80s teen cinema, there is no image more iconic than John Cusack holding up a boombox outside Ione Skye's bedroom blasting "In Your Eyes." This is such a powerful, romantic gesture, if Romeo had a boombox and a Peter Gabriel cassette, he and Juliet would still be alive. To Gen-X, no gesture embodies romance more than this moment. The opening few bars of this song will always be sure to melt any '80s girl's heart. It was Gabriel's finest moment and he didn't even need to bring along a team of Claymation animators.

Albums of the '80s:

Melt (1980)
Security (1982)
Birdy (1985)
So (1986)
Passion (1989)

The 11 Best Songs By Peter Gabriel:

1. **In Your Eyes** (*So*)
2. **Red Rain** (*So*)
3. **Games Without Frontiers** (*Melt*)
4. **I Don't Remember** (*Melt*)
5. **Don't Give Up** (*So*)
6. **Family Snapshot** (*Melt*)
7. **Shock The Monkey** (*Security*)
8. **I Have The Touch** (*Security*)
9. **Biko** (*Melt*)
10. **Sledgehammer** (*So*)
11. **Not One Of Us** (*Melt*)

Fun Fact: Peter Gabriel scored the movie *Last Temptation of Christ* directed by Martin Scorsese. The score was nominated for a Golden Globe and was nominated for two Grammys: Best Score Soundtrack and Best New Age Album. It won the Grammy for New Age Album.

Song Note (In Your Eyes): The song was inspired by an African tradition that plays with the line between love for another person and love for God.

GO-GO'S

The '80s were a groundbreaking decade for women. Sandra Day O'Connor became the first woman to serve on the United States Supreme Court. Sally Ride became the first American female astronaut, launching into space aboard the Space Shuttle Challenger. Geraldine Ferraro became the first female nominee to run for Vice President of the United States on a major party ticket. It was the decade where women became trailblazers and smashed through glass ceilings on the way to the stratosphere. The Go-Go's added their own female defining efforts to the social medium.

The Go-Go's made fun-loving, sugar pop rock music that celebrated life's spoils. On the surface, it appeared that these girls just wanted to have fun, but underneath, their music pushed forth a very strong message: female independence. The songs flowed with charisma and inner strength. They had bubble gum imagery on the surface but were more about the female experience and the challenges of the daily grind. Their songs connected with their target audience and their debut album, *Beauty and the Beat*, became a massive hit selling two million copies while spending six weeks on the top of the charts. The Go-Go's became the first female band who wrote their own songs and played their own instruments to accomplish this task. Being punk is about bucking the system. By dominating the charts making their own music, the Go-Go's punked them all and got all they really wanted.

Albums of the '80s:

Beauty and the Beat (1981)
Vacation (1982)
Talk Show (1984)

The 11 Best Songs By The Go-Go's:

1. **Our Lips Are Sealed** (*Beauty and the Beat*)
2. **Tonite** (*Beauty and the Beat*)
3. **We Don't Get Along** (*Vacation*)
4. **Vacation** (*Vacation*)
5. **Lust To Love** (*Beauty and the Beat*)
6. **Head Over Heels** (*Talk Show*)
7. **You Thought** (*Talk Show*)
8. **We Got The Beat** (*Beauty and the Beat*)
9. **I'm The Only One** (*Talk Show*)
10. **Speeding** (*Get Up and Go*)
11. **He's So Strange** (*Vacation*)

Fun Fact: The Go-Go's considered themselves a punk band and hated the way their debut album sounded. They even considered breaking up so they wouldn't have to play the songs live. When the album went double platinum, they changed their tune about it.

Song Note (Our Lips Are Sealed): This song was written by guitarist Jane Weidlin and singer Terry Hall of the Specials when the two bands toured together. The song is about the duo's brief secret romantic affair.

THE GRATEFUL DEAD

I would bet money that the biggest musical misconception from the '80s had to be that Jerry Garcia was the lead singer of the Grateful Dead. The Dead have a pot full of great legendary songs. Songs so popular that to this day they are often mistaken for being radio hits. When in fact, the Grateful Dead only had one radio hit, and it was in the 80s for "Touch of Grey." Though Jerry was lead singer on this track, throughout the band's career, he shared vocal duties with Bob Weir. To many fans, Bob Weir was the primary vocal force behind the Dead. But it wasn't just Bob and Jerry who carried the tunes; The Dead passed vocal duties around, like a fat joint filled with cosmic weed. In the '60s, Rod "Pigpen" McKernan sang with his Southern drawl on his blues-inspired tracks. The '70s had Donna Jean Godchaux and her effervescent charm. In the '80s, it was the keyboardist, Brent Mydland, who jumped on the microphone. While Jerry received all the glory in the media and MTV during the '80s, Mydland was receiving all the accolades during their live shows. Even with this new found mainstream attention, The Grateful Dead didn't care about the Top 40; they didn't care about popular success. Their goal was to take their "deadicated" fans on a long, strange trip. The live shows were what mattered most to them. Because of this, the Grateful Dead became the top-grossing live act of the decade. The Dead was all about being live.

Albums of the '80s:

Go To Heaven (1980)
In The Dark (1987)
Built To Last (1989)

The 11 Best Songs By The Grateful Dead:

1. **Touch of Grey** (*In The Dark*)
2. **Althea** (*Go To Heaven*)
3. **Throwing Stones** (*In The Dark*)
4. **Easy To Love You** (*Go To Heaven*)
5. **Foolish Heart** (*Built To Last*)
6. **Just A Little Light** (*Built To Last*)
7. **Black Muddy River** (*In The Dark*)
8. **Victim or the Crime** (*Built To Last*)
9. **Alabama Getaway** (*Go To Heaven*)
10. **Feel Like A Stranger** (*Go To Heaven*)
11. **My Brother Esau** (*In The Dark*)

Fun Fact: The Grateful Dead had a signature sound system called "The Wall of Sound." This sound system included over 600 speakers and required four trucks to transport. Because of its massive size and the length of time needed to set-up and tear down, the band had to have two separate set-ups. This way, while the band was playing a show, a separate road crew could be at the following location setting up for the next gig.

HALL & OATES

In the '80s, many people were suffering, and it was up to the musicians of the world to save them. Through a series of concerts and benefit singles, musicians did raise millions of dollars for charities like famine in Africa and struggling farmers in America. The causes were noble, and big guns like Paul McCartney, Bob Dylan, even a reunited Led Zeppelin showed up to help. Band Aid was a British supergroup of musicians featuring '80s icons like U2, Duran Duran, and Culture Club. USA for Africa was an American supergroup, featuring Michael Jackson, Billy Joel, Bruce Springsteen, and Lionel Richie. Both groups held massive benefit concerts with dozens of artists. Farm Aid featured both country and rock artists. If you never thought you'd see Alabama share a bill with Lou Reed, well, it happened.

Hall & Oates were present for all of it. They recorded with USA for Africa and performed at Live Aid and Farm Aid. They were the 1980s American do-gooders. With roots in doo-wop, R&B, and good old rock n' roll, Hall & Oates produced a massive string of hit singles, including twenty-eight top 40 hits and six number ones. Hall & Oates made undeniably charming music that you couldn't help but sing along with, even if you were wearing a Slayer T-shirt (granted, you'd have to be alone in your car to pull this off). Decades later, their music still holds up and the band was inducted into the Rock & Roll Hall of Fame. Sometimes nice guys do finish first.

Albums of the '80s:

Voices (1980)
Private Eyes (1981)
H20 (1982)
Big Bam Boom (1984)
Ooh Yeah! (1988)

The 11 Best Songs By Hall & Oates:

1. **You Make My Dreams Come True** (*Voices*)
2. **Private Eyes** (*Private Eyes*)
3. **Head Above Water** (*Private Eyes*)
4. **Kiss On My List** (*Voices*)
5. **Maneater** (*H20*)
6. **Out Of Touch** (*Big Bam Boom*)
7. **Cold Dark and Yesterday** (*Big Bam Boom*)
8. **Family Man** (*H20*)
9. **I Can't Go For That (No Can Do)** (*Private Eyes*)
10. **Say It Isn't So** (*Rock 'N Roll Part 1*)
11. **Delayed Reaction** (*H20*)

Fun Fact: Before they were a duo, Daryl Hall and John Oates competed against each other in a battle of the bands. When gang violence with gunfire broke out during the competition, Daryl and John took refuge in a service elevator. This is how they met.

THE HUMAN LEAGUE

I had a second home as a teenager; it was called The Mall. The mall was the closest thing we had to the internet. It's where we existed because it had everything we needed. We got our books from B. Dalton, we got our music from Sam Goody, and our movies from Suncoast. We got our video game fix at Aladdin's Castle arcade. Did you need a greeting card from Hallmark or a new toy from Kay-Bee? The mall had it covered. Most importantly, the mall is where we learned how to dress, not just pastel clothes from Contempo or jean overalls from Miller's Outpost but from the other humans who were shopping there just like you. The mall was a place where all shoppers co-existed under the same roof as one. It may have been the pantheon of capitalism, but the mall was the place that brought us all together.

The Human League is the ultimate mall band. Throwing on a pair of headphones and hearing songs like "Love Action" or "Don't You Want Me," can transport you back to the days of spending entire afternoons sitting on a bench, drinking an Orange Julius and shoving down a piece of Sbarro pizza, all the while doing nothing except watching the other customers walk around the mall. What made the Human League the soundtrack to mall life is that they had a genuine human warmth. They had tapped into that culture of humanity that needed to be around each other. Their music connected us together on a human level. The Human League was our human condition.

Albums of the '80s:

Holiday 80 (1980)
Travelogue (1980)
Dare (1981)
Fascination! (1983)
Hysteria (1984)
Crash (1986)

The 11 Best Songs By The Human League:

1. **Human** (*Crash*)
2. **Don't You Want Me** (*Dare*)
3. **Love Action** (*Dare*)
4. **Are You Ever Coming Back?** (*Crash*)
5. **Fascination** (*Fascination!*)
6. **The Things That Dreams Are Made Of** (*Dare*)
7. **Jam** (*Crash*)
8. **I Love You Too Much** (*Hysteria*)
9. **Seconds** (*Dare*)
10. **The Lebanon** (*Hysteria*)
11. **Do Or Die** (*Dare*)

Fun Fact: In the early '80s, keyboardists Ian Marsh and Martyn Ware quit the band to form Heaven 17. Singer Phil Oakey had three weeks to rebuild the band before they were scheduled to go on tour. Oakey found Susan Anne Sulley and Joanne Catherall dancing at a nightclub in Sheffield. Even though neither girl had sung or danced professionally, they both joined the band and have been the longest standing band members (besides Oakey) ever since.

HÜSKER DÜ

As a skateboarding fiend in the '80s, my Bible was Thrasher magazine. A skater's love for Thrasher mag was like belonging to an exclusive club. We bonded over high-flying 360-degree airs and balance-defying grinds (tricks I would try to mimic with very little success). I spent hours obsessing over its pages, cutting out photos for my bedroom wall. This was important business because you were judged by which Thrasher snapshots were pinned to your walls. As much as Thrasher magazine united skaters under one banner, there was another unifying force: punk rock. In fact, if you were a skater you weren't allowed to listen to anything other than punk rock. You better hope that one of your skater friends didn't find a Cyndi Lauper cassette in your closest or you would be ostracized faster than Ricky Schroder on *Silver Spoons* when he was grounded for experimenting with alcohol. Hüsker Dü was known for playing at blistering speeds with songs that rarely topped two minutes. Their songs emitted aggressive energy that was essential for any skate session. As the decade progressed, Hüsker Dü broadened their sound, diving into experimental rock, becoming more complex and introspective. Many fans abandoned them as they changed. What these fans didn't realize, the band was laying the foundations for what would become the alternative rock movement of the '90s. While skaters were busy celebrating the accomplishment of doing an ollie over a car, Hüsker Dü created a whole new genre of music.

Albums of the '80s:

Metal Circus (1983)
Everything Falls Apart (1983)
Zen Arcade (1984)
New Day Rising (1985)
Flip Your Wig (1985)
Sorry Somehow (1986)
Candy Apple Gray (1986)
Warehouse: Stories and Songs (1987)

The 11 Best Songs By Hüsker Dü:

1. **Something I Learned Today** (*Zen Arcade*)
2. **Don't Want To Know If You Are Lonely** (*Candy Apple Gray*)
3. **It's Not Funny Anymore** (*Metal Circus*)
4. **Terms of Psychic Warfare** (*New Day Rising*)
5. **Chartered Trips** (*Zen Arcade*)
6. **Could You Be One?** (*Warehouse: Songs and Stories*)
7. **Pink Turns To Blue** (*Zen Arcade*)
8. **Makes No Sense At All** (*Flip Your Wig*)
9. **Sorry Somehow** (*Candy Apple Gray*)
10. **Never Talking To You Again** (*Zen Arcade*)
11. **Visionary** (*Warehouse: Songs and Stories*)

Fun Fact: When the band broke up, bassist Greg Norton decided to leave the music industry to open his own restaurant called, The Norton's Restaurant. It broke up, too.

ICE-T

Colors was one of the most controversial movies to be released in the '80s. It was criticized by many for glamorizing gang violence. Despite the negative press, the film did well. As a teen, I was too young to see the film in its theatrical release. I had no choice but to wait a year for it to hit video. Some of the kids at school had older siblings who snuck them into the theater to see it. They said it was the most violent, bloodiest, darkest film ever. *The Faces of Death* videos were Saturday morning cartoons compared to the carnage in *Colors*. Months down the road, I managed to get a copy of the film. I waited until my parents had left the house and I sat down, ready to watch the most gruesome movie-going experience of all time. I hit play on the Betamax (yes, my parents owned a Betamax (∞)). I spent two hours watching a gritty police drama, waiting for horrifying scenes that never came. Instead, I watched Sean Penn playing an LA police officer dealing with gang crime in LA. That's all. I wouldn't be this disappointed in a film until the Star Wars prequels. One part of the movie that did not disappoint was the soundtrack, which was led by Ice-T's brazen title track. Ice-T's lyrics hit with brutal social reflection on inner city life. He was the voice of the drug pusher, the petty thief, the gang banger, the kid just trying to graduate high school. He didn't praise the criminal nature; he laid it out in such an insightful, introspective way that it was a shocking exposure to the struggles of urban life.

Albums of the '80s:

Rhyme Pays (1987)
Power (1988)
The Iceberg/Freedom of Speech...Just Watch What Say! (1989)

The 11 Best Songs By Ice-T:

1. **I'm Your Pusher** (*Power*)
2. **Colors** (*Colors Soundtrack*)
3. **Dog'N The Wax** (*Single*)
4. **You Played Yourself** (*The Iceberg/Freedom of Speech...Just Watch What Say!*)
5. **6 'n the Mornin'** (*Rhyme Pays*)
6. **Make It Funky** (*Rhyme Pays*)
7. **Power** (*Power*)
8. **Rhyme Pays** (*Rhyme Pays*)
9. **Radio Suckers** (*Power*)
10. **The Girl Tried To Kill Me** (*The Iceberg/Freedom of Speech...Just Watch What Say!*)
11. **Killers** (*Killers*)

Fun Fact: Ice-T would shed his gangster ways and start playing, of all things, a police detective on *Law & Order SVU*. For someone who was infamously hated by the police for his controversial song, "Cop Killer," he ironically went on to play a police detective for more years than any other actor ever.

(∞) **80s Note:** A Betamax video tape was the rival to the VHS. It was smaller and better quality but more expensive.

INXS

INXS' *Kick* was one of those albums that you couldn't escape. It was everywhere. In 1987–8, it was on every radio station; it was playing in every store. MTV didn't make it through a music video block without airing at least one video from the album. Every friend's car and every store in the mall had it playing. I was inundated by the howling voice of Michael Hutchence on whether he needed me, he mystified me, or he wanted to kick me. I cringed every time the sublime string section on "Never Tear Us Apart" percolated from nearby speakers. That song was always the doorway drug to a full sing-a-long by my friends, and many of them didn't even know the lyrics. I hated the album but not because I didn't like the music, it was because it had crept into every crevice of my world. Maybe it was the faux homage/blatant Bob Dylan rip-off in their video or the way that Hutchence's hair flopped around like he just took a bath in a tub full of Pert Plus. Whatever it was, I wanted to take the album to a Thuggee temple and sacrifice it. But I admit, I was wrong. There was a reason the album had infiltrated every aspect of society. The album was exceptional. Twenty years later, when the '80s veneer had worn off, I finally found an appreciation for it. It was through of all things, Beck's Record Club. Beck, St. Vincent, and The Liars combined forces and covered the whole album *Kick*. Because of my love for Beck and friends, it reopened my ears to how good INXS was. So good, that I played it until I got my kids to fall in love with it, too.

Albums of the '80s:

INXS (1980)
Underneath the Colours (1981)
Shabooh Shoobah (1982)
The Swing (1984)
Listen Like Thieves (1985)
Kick (1987)

The 11 Best Songs By INXS:

1. **Never Tear Us Apart** (*Kick*)
2. **Don't Change** (*Shabooh Shoobah*)
3. **Kick** (*Kick*)
4. **Original Sin** (*The Swing*)
5. **Mystify** (*Kick*)
6. **Listen Like Thieves** (*Listen Like Thieves*)
7. **Need You Tonight/Mediate** (*Kick*)
8. **On a Bus** (*INXS*)
9. **Soul Mistake** (*Shabooh Shoobah*)
10. **Kiss The Dirt** (*Listen Like Thieves*)
11. **What You Need** (*Listen Like Thieves*)

Fun Fact: The video for INXS' "Need You Tonight/Mediate," which borrows heavily from Bob Dylan's "Subterranean Homesick Blues," swept the 1988 MTV video music awards, winning five awards including Video of the Year.

IRON MAIDEN

The '80s were filled with rivalries. Lakers vs. Celtics. Coke vs. Pepsi. David Lee Roth vs. Sammy Hagar. General Lee vs. K.I.T.T. Topps vs. Fleer. No rivalry struck harder at the hearts of teenage metalheads than Iron Maiden vs. Judas Priest. Asking a metal fan to pick between the two bands is like asking Philip Drummond who his favorite son was. Arnold is a knee-jerk pick, but Willis is really the one who had his shit together. Here, I will argue that Iron Maiden is the best. Iron Maiden was the champion of the new wave of British metal. With classically trained musicians and a twin guitar attack, Maiden infused punk anarchy, to craft songs that were metal perfection. Lead singer Bruce Dickinson was the ultimate metal frontman. With his guitar shop hair, tight leather pants, ripped shirts exposing ample chest hair, and a battle-torn face, Bruce looked like he was made in a metal laboratory in the depths of hell. Maiden had an insane streak of genre-defining albums that spanned across the entire decade. Radio play meant nothing to them, nor did it need to as they would go on to sell 80 million albums worldwide. What gives Maiden an edge is that their songs created fantastical worlds that would transport the introverted dreamer to new realms of imagination. These macabre dreams spilled onto their stage show that was a spectacle of cryptic proportions. Iron Maiden didn't dominate because they were the best metal band, they dominated because they took metal and turned it up to eleven.

Albums of the '80s:

Iron Maiden (1980)
Killers (1981)
Number of the Beast (1982)
Piece of Mind (1983)
Powerslave (1984)
Somewhere In Time (1986)
Seventh Son of A Seventh Son (1988)

The 11 Best Songs By Iron Maiden:

1. **Hallowed Be Thy Name** (*Number of the Beast*)
2. **22 Acacia Avenue** (*Number of the Beast*)
3. **Killers** (*Killers*)
4. **Number Of The Beast** (*Number of the Beast*)
5. **The Trooper** (*Piece of Mind*)
6. **The Evil That Men Do** (*Seventh Son of A Seventh Son*)
7. **Can I Play With Madness** (*Seventh Son of A Seventh Son*)
8. **2 Minutes To Midnight** (*Powerslave*)
9. **Rime of the Ancient Mariner** (*Powerslave*)
10. **Run To The Hills** (*Number of the Beast*)
11. **Prowler** (*Iron Maiden*)

Fun Fact: The band has a fictional mascot, named Eddie The Head. Eddie is a zombie-like figure that appears on all of their album covers and is usually a gigantic fixture featured as a part of their concerts.

Set-Break/Defending La Toya Jackson

On May 16, 1983, Michael Jackson changed the world. That was the day that NBC aired the music special, *Motown 25: Yesterday, Today, Forever*. During Michael Jackson's performance of "Billie Jean," the sequined-glove wearing superstar, pulled up his pants, shook his head and gracefully Moonwalked across the stage. That 3-second Moonwalk is legendary. It is the inciting event that launched Michael into superstardom stratosphere, crowning himself the King of Pop and bringing his whole family with him as American royalty.

As the clocked ticked into 1980, there was no doubt in anyone's mind that Michael Jackson was a star. As the lead vocalist in The Jackson 5 (and later the Jacksons when the group moved to Sony/Epic) the world was already in love with Michael's innocent, charismatic charm. When he performed, he was a natural. A pure born entertainer. He commanded a stage with such natural talent, it was mesmerizing to watch. His dance moves were effortless, flawless, like watching a bird in flight. The only entertainers who could compare to Michael's incredible stage presence were Fred Astaire and Elvis Presley. That's some good company. Then, you have Michael's voice. When he sang, it was like butter. He emoted from the heart. If he sang a love song, you felt his compassion. That's saying a lot considering he was just a teenager who probably had never been in love. His vocal control was otherworldly. His ability to manipulate his octave range to reach Icarus-level highs and earth-pounding lows was so masterful, it was like he wasn't even human. The way he could throw in vocal hiccups, stutters, and stops without losing a beat was like watching Mary Lou Retton score a perfect ten in the 1984 Olympics in gymnastics. And this is what we thought of him before we heard *Thriller*.

Michael Jackson's voice and style were so distinct, a single "woo" was a beacon of light in a darkened room. He brought magic to our world. He brought songs that will live forever. But Michael was not alone. Michael had siblings. Many of them. Michael had eight siblings: five brothers and three sisters. His five brothers are Jackie, Jermaine, Marlon, Randy, and Tito. His three sisters are Rebbie, Janet, and La Toya. Every single one of his siblings were or still are involved in music. Every single one of them has their own solo album. Granted it took Tito until 2017 to release his first solo album, *Tito Time*...but he did it. Every single one of Michael's siblings is musically talented but one of them has spent more time under a critical light than in the limelight. That would be La Toya. She has been kicked out of her family, shamed in the press, and ridiculed as a joke. But did she deserve it?

There is more talent pulsing through the Jackson family veins than anyone would think possible. This is why the Jackson 5 were so astounding when they came onto the scene. Every single brother was bursting with natural talent. It was a super group of R&B stars before they were stars. Their musical prowess was so intense, the outpouring of music couldn't be contained. They released nine albums in just six years. They were the first group to have their first four singles go to number one on the charts, and seven singles reached the top ten. Their number one song, "ABC," knocked the Beatles "Let It Be" out of the number one spot.

Talk about symbolic. The Jackson 5 were so beloved, they had their own variety show on CBS, their own Saturday morning cartoon, board games, and everything in between. Jacksonmania was real.

Due to the band's overwhelming popularity, both Michael and Jermaine embarked on solo careers in the middle of the mania. While Michael's music still embodied a lot of his childlike persona, Jermaine set himself apart with a more mature approach to his music. It worked. Jermaine became a worthy solo artist on par with Michael. This was one of the many reasons why Jermaine stayed behind to record with Motown when the Jackson 5 left to record with Sony/Epic. The Jackson 5 had their heyday in the '70s, but the move to Sony/Epic is the moment that set up the family for domination in the '80s.

The Jacksons owned the '80s. I don't mean that in a metaphorical sense, I mean in every sense. From 1980 to 1989, the Jackson clan released twenty-six albums, over one hundred singles, selling over sixty million albums in the US and over one hundred million albums worldwide. They led massive sold out tours everywhere. The Jacksons weren't just American royalty, they were American superheroes.

In fourth grade, I used to come home after school and turn on the TV in my parents' bedroom (which was the only TV in the house that had cable). At 3:00 PM every day, MTV would air Michael Jackson's epic 14-minute video for "Thriller." I made sure I was home in time to see it, every single day. I had swarms of friends who didn't have cable, begging me to come over so they could watch it, too. "Thriller" was unlike any song ever made. It was a genre unto itself. It was a horror song. It had pop sensibilities but still managed to creep into your soul and give you a scare. It was as addictive as it was frightening. Everyone had Jacksonmania. Kids wore sequined gloves. Girls dreamed of growing up to marry Michael. Michael Jackson's *Thriller* was more than a phenomenon, it was in our DNA as a society.

In retrospect, there is very little doubt that after Michael, Janet Jackson's solo career was a close second. That said, heading into the '80s, Janet was considered the least likely to find success. Jermaine had found a formidable niche, veering into classic R&B. He had a solid output of grounded, pulse-pounding music. With six albums released in the '80s, Jermaine was by far the most productive of the siblings. "Let's Get Serious" is a bona fide jam. And it didn't hurt that Jermaine had input from Stevie Wonder, Herbie Hancock, and even Devo. Jermaine's musical acuity was so respected, he was hired to produce Whitney Houston's debut album, *Whitney Houston*.

The rest of the brothers (Randy, Tito, Jackie, and Marlon) were still cranking out quality hits as The Jacksons, with help from little brother Michael and The Rolling Stones' Mick Jagger. They launched two sold out mega tours for their albums, *Triumph* and *Victory*. Meanwhile, older sister, Rebbie, teamed up with Michael to release her biggest hit, "Centipede," establishing her own respectable solo career.

It wasn't until 1986, when Janet released *Control* that she took control of her career. Shedding the bubble gum pop sound of her first two albums, *Control* was a statement of female empowerment and struck a heavy nerve with women, who immediately took up Janet's rallying cry. Six million albums later, Janet had proved that she was every bit a Jackson. As the decade came to an end, Janet released her socially conscious, *Rhythm Nation 1814*. Inspired by the likes of Bob Dylan and Marvin Gaye, Janet created a movement of unity. It was about bringing together people of all races, all sexes, and all nationalities. Eight million albums later, Janet was no longer living in Michael's shadow, she was casting her own.

In the beginning of the decade, it wasn't Janet, Jermaine, or even Rebbie that was seen as the next heavyweight in the Jackson family. Believe it or not, it was La Toya. La Toya had albums with style and personality, she was poised to establish her own career. By the end of the decade, La Toya was an afterthought, an outcast, a reject. But why?

Now, I'm not looking to claim that La Toya was the best of her family, that she was better than Michael, Janet, Jermaine, or even Tito (*Tito Time* is an unexpectedly good album). Taste is arbitrary. Whether a listener enjoys La Toya's music is up to the listener to decide. What I am focusing in on is why La Toya went from being the rising star of the Jackson clan to being kicked out of her own family. She did have some questionable public antics but was she the perpetrator or the victim?

In the '80s, La Toya was a respected artist in her own right. She was her own brand. Over the course of five albums, she had nine singles that charted on the R&B charts. Her biggest hit, "Heart Don't Lie" from the album of the same name featured Howard Hewitt, lead singer of Shalamar and music by Musical Youth. In fact, many of La Toya's songs featured big names jumping in to lend a hand. Whether it was Stevie Wonder playing harmonica, Ray Parker Jr. busting guitars instead of ghosts, Toto's Jeff Pocaro beating the drums, Kool & The Gang funking up the tracks, or any of her siblings laying down some vocals, there was no short supply of talented artists wanting to join in on the good times. La Toya was so well respected, she started writing songs for reggae star, Jimmy Cliff. La Toya's song, "Reggae Nights" was such a hit for Cliff, the song was nominated for a Grammy. If that wasn't good enough, she would write two more songs for Cliff's next album that would go onto win the Grammy for best reggae album. That's right, La Toya Jackson is a Grammy winning reggae songwriter. But wait, there's more.

In the mid-80s, fashion designer and leather specialist, David Laurenz would create an entire line of clothes just for La Toya, including a line of signature headbands. La Toya would become the face and spokesperson for Nikon cameras. She even had her own fragrance called of all things: La Toya. And to top it all off, La Toya was asked to participate in the mammoth charity single, "We Are the World." Sure, Michael was one of the producers, but Janet didn't make the cut.

So, where did it all go wrong? It comes down to one man: Jack Gordon. Gordon was originally brought in to manage La Toya but would end up taking over her entire career trajectory, which he sent plummeting into the ground. One of the first social missteps that Gordon pushed on La Toya was posing for Playboy. Being one of the most conservative of her family, seeing La Toya engage in such an expose left her family in a state of shock. Bo Derek, Kim Basinger, Brooke Shields, Goldie Hawn, and even Madonna all posed in Playboy but none of them received the level of scrutiny that La Toya did. Gordon's influence didn't stop there.

Gordon pushed La Toya into joining the Moulin Rouge cabaret dinner theater in Paris, writing a tell-all autobiography about her family, and becoming the host of the Psychic Friends Network. Every one of these pursuits would slowly tear down her image and respectability. How did Gordon convince La Toya to do all these unflattering things? Easy. He beat the crap out of her.

Gordon routinely physically, mentally and emotionally abused La Toya into doing what he wanted her to do, including marrying him. One time Gordon beat her so bad, he thought he had killed her. When he realized she might be dead, he didn't call for an ambulance, instead, he called his friends to brag that he had just killed La Toya Jackson. Let me repeat: Jack Gordon thought he had beaten La Toya Jackson to death so he called his friends to brag about it. This was La Toya's life. This was her everyday situation. This is why she couldn't say no to his suggestions. For years, no matter how hard she tried, she couldn't escape. But the story has a happy ending.

Eventually, little brother Randy Jackson came to the rescue and helped La Toya escape from Gordon and file for divorce. By then, La Toya had almost nothing left of the career she had built in the '80s. Since then, she has been brought back into the Jackson fold and was even the spokesperson for the family when Michael died.

What La Toya represents is bigger than what she was. She was the collateral damage of her family's fame, the victim for Michael's stardom, and the consequence for Janet's movement. More than that, she lived the nightmare that all women fear. What Gordon did to her was about sexism, oppression and control. A common theme in the underbelly of the '80s. From the posters on bedroom walls to girls dancing in videos, women were viewed as objects. They were the prize of celebrity. They were the achievement.

And if they fought back, they were punished and labeled as crazy rather than the victim.

The disrespect of women in the '80s goes much deeper than just being objects of sexual gratification. The deeper sentiment is that women were lesser beings. They were meant for the entertainment of men. They weren't viewed as people capable of having their own ideas or feelings. Don't believe me, go back and watch some '80s movies. In *Weird Science*, Robert Downey, Jr. tries to trade his girlfriend for a hotter girl. In *Meatballs*, Bill Murray dry humps a girl against her will. In *Monster Squad*, a kid uses a naked picture of his friend's sister as black mail. Women were not equal.

Aretha demanded respect. Tina said you better be good to her. And even though, Janet proclaimed her nastiness, it was all about taking control back. Now it's La Toya's turn. If we can change our perception then, we can finally give La Toya the respect she deserves.

What the Jacksons represent is more than just great music, there's a socially conscious thread through their existence and domination. From the racially charged '60s, the Jacksons emerged as a force of unification for all people no matter your race. In the '80s, the Jacksons once again became the voice for the underappreciated as Janet and La Toya became the voices for women needing to be heard.

Whether it was the message, the movement, the emotion, the passion, or just the harmony of the music, the Jacksons gave this world the ultimate gift, they gave themselves.

THE JACKSONS

Cabbage Patch Kids were the most popular toy fad of the decade. The Cabbage Patch Brand made almost 2 billion dollars per year. Cabbage Patch Kids may have been just a doll but they were the doll that did it the best. On Christmas Eve, 1983, I sat in the back of my mom's car, staring out the window at the infestation of cars clogging the mall parking lot as folks made a mad rush to get one last special item for under the tree. We were no different. My mom wanted a gift from the toy store for our neighbor's kid, but we couldn't even get into the parking lot due to the hoards of cars vying for a spot. More shocking was the line of people waiting to get into the store. It stretched across the lot and wrapped around the corner. They were waiting for the hottest toy on the planet: a Cabbage Patch Kid.

The Jacksons were the best. There is no doubt that the 80s belonged to the Jackson Family. Michael dominated. Janet dominated. Jermaine, La Toya, Rebbie, and even Marlon burned up the dance floors. Their family sold over 100 million albums worldwide. Their songs ruled the charts. Their concerts sold out faster than a fresh supply of Cabbage Patch Kids. You had a better chance of beating Mike Tyson in Punch-Out than getting a ticket to a Jackson show. All this happened for one simple thing: they made great music. The Jacksons were always in front blazing the path for dance, disco, R&B, and everything that just made you feel good because they made music that came from the heart and soul.

Albums of the '80s:

Triumph (1980)
The Jacksons Live! (1981)
Victory (1984)
2300 Jackson Street (1989)

The 11 Best Songs By The Jacksons:

1. **Torture** (*Victory*)
2. **Can You Feel It** (*Triumph*)
3. **This Place Hotel** (*Triumph*)
4. **Everybody** (*Triumph*)
5. **Art of Madness** (*2300 Jackson Street*)
6. **Lovely One** (*Triumph*)
7. **Wait** (*Victory*)
8. **State of Shock** (*Victory*)
9. **The Hurt** (*Victory*)
10. **Your Ways** (*Triumph*)
11. **2300 Jackson Street** (*2300 Jackson Street*)

Fun Fact: Michael Jackson recorded three song with Freddie Mercury in preparation for the *Victory* album. They were "There Must Be More To Life Than This," "Victory," and "State of Shock." The last song would be re-recorded with Mick Jagger filling in for Mercury. Of the three Freddie Mercury duets, only "There Must Be More To Life Than This" was officially released.

JESUS AND THE MARY CHAIN

As the older brother in my family, I didn't have an elder sibling like John Cusack in *Stand By Me* to educate me on what was cool. My parents were little help. The coolest thing my parents listened to were The Beatles or Quicksilver Messenger Service. Both are respectable bands but not helpful in keeping me musically cool in the 80s. The only way I could keep up with new music was through my friends. I found out about JMC when my buddy was playing *Darklands* in his car. He said, "This is the band that will change the world." That's high praise for any band. The next time I was at the mall, I made a trip to Sam Goody. *Barbed Wire Kisses* was the only JMC album available, so I purchased it. Back then, buying an album without hearing it was very common. I was not immediately impressed. It felt all over the place and disjointed. I didn't realize it was a B-sides album. I stuffed it away without another listen. It wasn't until the JMC put out their fuzzed-out rocker, *Automatic*, that I gave the band another listen. This time I fell deep into the rabbit hole of their early albums. It was reverb heaven. Hidden under the static was a 60s beach groove that echoed through the songs like a Gothic siren. From there, the songs exploded into a Timothy Leary-influenced cataclysm that made every song feel like the walls all around you were shaking with psychedelic energy. Changing the world may have been overly strong praise, but the JMC did have the power to alter the world around me.

Albums of the '80s:

Psychocandy (1985)
Darklands (1987)
Barbed Wire Kisses (1988)
Automatic (1989)

The 11 Best Songs By Jesus And The Mary Chain:

1. **Between Planets** (*Automatic*)
2. **Happy When It Rains** (*Darklands*)
3. **Darklands** (*Darklands*)
4. **Head On** (*Automatic*)
5. **Don't Ever Change** (*Barbed Wire Kisses*)
6. **A Taste of Cindy** (*Psychocandy*)
7. **Down On Me** (*Darklands*)
8. **Coast To Coast** (*Automatic*)
9. **Rider** (*Darklands* EP)
10. **Never Understand** (*Psychocandy*)
11. **Everything's Alright When You're Down** (*Happy When It Rains*)

Fun Fact: During one of their shows, fans threw beer bottles at the band, unhappy with their performance. This was exaggerated in the press, which claimed that the band had instigated a riot. They were tagged, "The New Sex Pistols," and because of this, they were banned from playing in certain townships.

JOAN JETT

As a youngster, I lived and breathed sitcom reruns from the moment I got out of school until dinner time. I knew the people in my shows better than the people in my house. These characters became my family. I knew all of Sam Malone's stats, I knew all Jack Tripper's roommates, Punky Brewster was always getting me into trouble, and Jo Polniaczek was my girlfriend. She just didn't know it yet, but when we'd eventually meet, and she'd be wearing my letterman jacket. Most importantly, Alex P. Keaton was the wise older brother I never had. I worshipped Michael J. Fox. When he made the movie, *Light of Day*, co-starring Joan Jett, I was at the theater on opening weekend. I went to see Michael; I left in love with Joan. She lit up screen with such scorching charisma I completely forgot that I was there to see her co-star. She was the baddest, toughest, most amazing woman I had ever seen rock a stage. If I was fighting a Russian invasion, I wanted Joan Jett as my back up. If I were going into the Fire Swamp to take on an R.O.U.S., I would want Joan Jett as my guide. Joan Jett made a career of doing everything her way, from refusing to exploit herself to sell records to starting her own label when every other label in town turned her down. Joan Jett is not a badass. Whatever is better than badass, Joan Jett is ten levels above that. A badass is someone who *listens* to Joan Jett. Joan Jett is so cool her music turns people into badasses. Joan Jett's legacy is one of inspiration, perspiration, and courage, leaving a permanent influence on female rockers for decades to come.

Albums of the '80s:

Bad Reputation (1981)
I Love Rock N' Roll (1981)
Album (1983)
Glorious Results of a Misspent Youth (1984)
Good Music (1986)
Up Your Alley (1988)

The 11 Best Songs By Joan Jett:

1. **Bad Reputation** (*Bad Reputation*)
2. **Victim of Circumstance** (*I Love Rock N' Roll*)
3. **I'm Gonna Run Away** (*I Love Rock N' Roll*)
4. **Had Enough** (*Album*)
5. **Push and Stomp** (*Glorious Results of a Misspent Youth*)
6. **I Hate Myself For Loving You** (*Up Your Alley*)
7. **Do You Wanna Touch Me (Oh Yeah)** (*Bad Reputation*)
8. **Handyman** (*Album*)
9. **Secret Love** (*Album*)
10. **Make Believe** (*Bad Reputation*)
11. **You Want In, I Want Out** (*Up Your Alley*)

Fun Fact: Joan Jett first recorded "I Love Rock N' Roll" in 1979 (which is why it doesn't make my list). Her backing band on the song was Steve Jones and Paul Cook of the Sex Pistols. So if you ever wondered what the Sex Pistols would have sounded like with a female singer...she'd sound like Joan Jett.

JOURNEY

I was introduced to Journey through the most infectious invention of the eighties: video games. The Atari 2600 was the first home video game system that the general public could buy. Besides *Yars Revenge,* most of the Atari 2600 games were garbage in comparison to the games that would be released in later years. We didn't know any better at the time, so any video game was a technological achievement of epic proportions. Especially the *E.T.* video game. I loved playing it even though it was a giant step backward for humankind. Conceptually, the Journey video game was completely bonkers. In the game, you controlled members of the band as they ran up a scrolling screen, dodging groupies, paparazzi, and guys who looked like the pile of shit Bill Paxton turns into at the end of *Weird Science.* If you successfully maneuvered all five band members to their Journey mobile, they would jettison to the next concert. Even though the concept was completely dull, it was as addictive as crack. I used to go to my friend's house to watch his older brother play that game for hours. I wanted him to get all the members to their vehicle so I could see the amateurishly animated cut scene of the vehicle flying through space. But my friend's brother was terrible at video games. So, he never did it. One night at a sleepover, I snuck into the living room and played that game faithfully for hours until finally, I conquered it. It was a dream. From that moment forward I learned if you never stop believing, you could have it any way you want it.

Albums of the '80s:

Departure (1980)
Dream, After Dream (1980)
Escape (1981)
Frontiers (1983)
Raised On Radio (1986)

The 11 Best Songs By Journey:

1. **Don't Stop Believin'** (*Escape*)
2. **Separate Ways** (*Frontiers*)
3. **Ask The Lonely** (*Two of a Kind*)
4. **Only The Young** (*Vision Quest*)
5. **Faithfully** (*Frontiers*)
6. **Who's Crying Now** (*Escape*)
7. **Open Arms** (*Escape*)
8. **Girl Can't Help It** (*Raised On Radio*)
9. **Edge of the Blade** (*Frontiers*)
10. **Stone In Love** (*Escape*)
11. **Send Her My Love** (*Frontiers*)

Fun Fact: Bassist, Randy Jackson, recorded and toured with the band for one album, *Raised On The Radio*. Years down the road in the 2000s, Randy would go on to host a little-known TV show called *American Idol*.

Song Note (Don't Stop Believin'): The chorus for the song and the first mention of the title of the song do not occur until the final 30 seconds of the song.

JUDAS PRIEST

The 80s were filled with rivalries. Star Wars vs. Star Trek. Burger King vs. McDonald's. Nintendo vs. Sega. Nike vs. Reebok. Freddy vs. Jason. No rivalry struck harder at the hearts of teenage metalheads than that of Iron Maiden vs. Judas Priest. Asking a metal fan to pick between the two bands is comparable to asking Sam Malone who his favorite waitress was. Though Diane is the popular pick, Rebecca was way less crazy. Here I will argue for Judas Priest. Priest wins by a kilometer because they invented the genre. They invented metal. They invented the twin guitar attack that Maiden pilfered. The leather attire with metal spikes that every metal band ever wore, that came from lead singer Rob Halford's fashion explosion. And while we're on the subject of Rob, no one... and I mean no one can match his signature scream. Many have tried (Axl Rose came close), but they all fall short. What elevates Priest's music is that they were bringing in influences from all of rock, from blues to roots. And while Maiden has a sweltering legion of metal fans, Judas Priest has more non-metal fans. While Maiden is the king of escapism, Priest is grounded in realism. Priest's ballads have a true range of human emotion that allows them to connect with their audience on a personal level. Not that Priest needs to find more ways to connect with their audience; seeing Halford ride around the stage on a motorcycle is about as metal as you can get. While there is an argument to be made that Iron Maiden was the best metal band in the '80s, Judas Priest wins as the all-time greatest.

Albums of the '80s:

British Steel (1980)

Point of Entry (1981)

Screaming for Vengeance (1982)

Defenders of the Faith (1984)

Turbo (1986)

Ram It Down (1988)

The 11 Best Songs By Judas Priest:

1. **Living After Midnight** (*British Steel*)
2. **You've Got Another Thing Coming** (*Screaming for Vengeance*)
3. **Breakin' The Law** (*British Steel*)
4. **Heading Out to the Highway** (*Point of Entry*)
5. **The Sentinel** (*Defenders of the Faith*)
6. **Some Heads are Gonna Roll** (*Defenders of the Faith*)
7. **Screaming for Vengeance** (*Screaming for Vengeance*)
8. **Electric Eye** (*Screaming For Vengeance*)
9. **Love Bites** (*Defenders of the Faith*)
10. **Hot Rockin'** (*Point of Entry*)
11. **Metal Gods** (*British Steel*)

Fun Fact: The name of the band comes from the Bob Dylan song, "The Ballad of Frankie Lee and Judas Priest." The term "Judas Priest" was commonly used by actors onscreen instead of using the term, "Jesus Christ," as to not offend anyone in the audience.

THE GREG KIHN BAND

Ever heard of Michael Dukakis? Walter Mondale? Gary Hart? You haven't? I'm sure for anyone who didn't come of age in the '80s (or even some of us who did) it might be a little surprising to learn that these men were a handful of votes away from being the next President of the United States. By losing the election, these men faded into obscurity, with their legacy being nothing more than their names in a history book with an asterisk next to them. For the rest of time, they will always be known as the "other guy." Being the other guy doesn't mean you're the wrong guy or the bad guy. You're the overlooked guy, the underrated guy, the underappreciated guy. Though they lost the election, they still achieved the second greatest honor out there; and to half the country, they were the number one pick.

Greg Kihn is rock's other guy. Always the opening act but never the headliner. He's too east coast to be Tom Petty, but not east coast enough to be Bruce Springsteen. He's too blue collar to be Billy Joel, but too suburban to be John Cougar. He's too mainstream rock to be David Bowie, but too alternative to be Rick Springfield. He has too much '50s to be Bob Dylan, but too much '60s to be Elvis. This isn't a list of everything that Greg Kihn isn't; this is a list of everything he is. Kihn pulled influence from everywhere, mixing it all into punchy street-level rock n' roll. He didn't have had one distinct sound that set him apart, instead his music incorporated all the sounds into one.

Albums of the '80s:

Glass House Rock (1980)
Rockihnroll (1981)
Kihntinued (1982)
Kihnspiracy (1983)
Kihntagious (1984)
Citizen Kihn (1985)
Love and Rock and Roll (1986)

The 11 Best Songs By The Greg Kihn Band:

1. **The Breakup Song (They Don't Write 'Em)** (*Rockihnroll*)
2. **Can't Stop Hurting Myself** (*Rockihnroll*)
3. **The Worst That Could Happen** (*Kihntagious*)
4. **Seeing Is Believing** (*Kihntinued*)
5. **Fascination** (*Kihnspiracy*)
6. **Jeopardy** (*Kihnspiracy*)
7. **How Long** (*Kihnspiracy*)
8. **Boys Won't** (*Citizen Kihn*)
9. **They Rock The Night** (*Citizen Kihn*)
10. **Night After Night** (*Glass House Rock*)
11. **Go Back** (*Citizen Kihn*)

Fun Fact: Though Kihn prides himself on being a straight-forward rocker, the videos for his songs "Jeopardy" and "Reunited" are a two-part fantasy/sci-fi tale that includes dreams within dreams, "Thriller"-esque zombies, and a journey to the magical land of Oz, with more subtext and complexity than all of Terry Gilliam's movies combined.

LET'S ACTIVE

Most people have no idea who Let's Active is; but here's a bold statement: in the beginning of the jangle pop movement, Let's Active was a better band than R.E.M. While R.E.M. is viewed as the ambassador of jangle pop, the bands that proliferated that scene were some of the most intriguing yet overlooked bands of the entire decade. While there's no argument that R.E.M. was the most famous jangle pop group, they weren't the only one. Jangle pop was the dominant musical genre of the Southern U.S., and, it sounds exactly as described: jangly, 12-string guitars that create a warbly, almost psychedelic vibe with vocals that share the same imperfections. Influenced by '60s folk, jangle pop was the true ground floor of the indie/college rock universe. Let's Active never reached commercial success like R.E.M., but in their southern domain, both bands were considered equals, playing on many of the same bills. In fact, Let's Active's first live gig was the opening act for R.E.M. Eventually, Michael Stipe's mumble and Peter Buck's rumbling melodies catapulted R.E.M. to stardom, but most fans of the scene thought Let's Active with their addictive hooks and full throttle passion would be the breakout success. Though R.E.M.'s exhaustive catalog puts them on top today, when the two bands started out, it was Let's Active who was paving the way. Without Let's Active, there may never have been R.E.M. Their inclusion in this book is that attempt to get them the notoriety they deserve.

Albums of the '80s:

Afoot (1983)
Cypress (1984)
Big Plans For Everybody (1986)
Every Dog Has His Day (1988)

The 11 Best Songs By Let's Active:

1. **Every Word Means No** (*Afoot EP*)
2. **Blue Line** (*Cypress*)
3. **Room With A View** (*Afoot EP*)
4. **Ring True** (*Cypress*)
5. **Talking To Myself** (*Big Plans For Everybody*)
6. **Fell** (*Big Plans For Everybody*)
7. **Reflecting Pool** (*Big Plans For Everybody*)
8. **Flags For Everything** (*Cypress*)
9. **Every Dog Has His Day** (*Every Dog Has His Day*)
10. **Ten Layers Down** (*Every Dog Has His Day*)
11. **Counting Down** (*Cypress*)

Fun Fact: Mitch Easter, lead singer of Let's Active, was the producer on R.E.M.'s first EP (*Chronic Town*) and first two albums (*Murmur* and *Reckoning*).

LL COOL J

In the eighties, everything was about being "cool." If you wanted to be seen driving a cool vehicle, you better show up to the club in an Italian sports car whose doors lift upwards like it can travel back in time. If you wanted to wear cool sunglasses, then they needed to be brightly neon-colored. If you wanted to wear cool jeans, then you better buy them at the Guess store. (Hey, that's all we had back then!) But no artist oozed cool better than rapper, LL Cool J, the coolest artist to every stroll across the music video screen.

LL Cool J was so cool, he redefined what it meant to be cool. It was no longer about stain-washed jeans and fluorescent colors; LL dressed up by dressing down. He wore designer work-out gear like he was on the way to the gym if he felt like it. Sometimes he didn't even bother to wear a shirt...and he didn't need to. The guy was ripped. He wasn't a lazy rock star who was on the beer and cocaine diet; he was on the 3-hours at the gym diet. LL cared about how he looked, and the ladies loved him for it. LL was a bad ass, but he was also a sensitive guy. He was tougher than a muscle-bound man but soft enough to lay down a jacket so you could walk over a puddle. His lyrics embodied all of this. They were empowering indictments of personal strength. While many rappers preached revolution in society, LL spat lyrics urging that revolution comes from inner strength. LL was that type of guy. Why do you think all the ladies love cool James?

Albums of the '80s:

Radio (1985)
Bigger and Deffer (1987)
Walking With A Panther (1989)

The 11 Best Songs By LL Cool J:

1. **Going Back To Cali** (*Walking With A Panther*)
2. **I'm Bad** (*Bigger and Deffer*)
3. **Rock the Bells** (*Radio*)
4. **I Can't Live Without My Radio** (*Radio*)
5. **.357 - Break It On Down** (*Bigger and Deffer*)
6. **I'm That Type of Guy** (*Walking With A Panther*)
7. **Ahh, Let's Get Ill** (*Bigger and Deffer*)
8. **That's A Lie** (*Radio*)
9. **Droppin' Em** (*Walking With A Panther*)
10. **Jack The Ripper** (*Walking With A Panther*)
11. **Dangerous** (*Radio*)

Fun Fact: LL Cool J's biological great-uncle was Hall of Fame boxer, John Henry Lewis.

Song Note (Going Back To Cali): Though it's assumed that the song refers to LL's refusal to go back to California, the double meaning in the song is that he's actually singing about his ex-girlfriend (named Cali) and he is trying to keep himself from running back to her.

LOVE AND ROCKETS

As a young boy, I lived in the constant debilitating fear of the world ending at any moment due to a nuclear holocaust. I didn't follow politics, and we didn't have world leaders trading snarky insults via social media like middle school kids; we just knew that the United States and the Soviet Union had so many nuclear missiles that they could blow up the Earth ten times over and still have enough firepower to take out the moon and at least half of Mars. With post-apocalyptic movies like *The Day After* or the Mad Max films, I, and I'm sure most of my generation, felt the end of the world was always right around the corner. Maybe that's why life in the '80s was so carefree. We lived life to the fullest because we thought we could all die at any minute.

Love and Rockets were formed out of the ashes of the Bauhaus break-up, retaining all of the Bauhaus members minus singer Peter Murphy. Without the restraints of the expectations that came with being the Bauhaus, Love and Rockets became looser with their music. Still channeling the essence of goth, the band gracefully floated into the pop sphere with an armload of new tales to tell. Drawing on influences from the likes of the Beatles and T. Rex, Love and Rockets reinvented their image from being one mired in darkness to celebrating being so alive. Love and Rockets' songs were explosions of creative complexity that challenged typical pop arrangements but were as seductive as a heavenly teenage dream.

Albums of the '80s:

Seventh Dream of a Teenage Heaven (1985)
Express (1986)
Earth, Sun, Moon (1987)
Love and Rockets (1989)

The 11 Best Songs By Love And Rockets:

1. **All In My Mind** (*Express*)
2. **Life in Laralay** (*Express*)
3. **No New Tale To Tell** (*Earth, Sun, Moon*)
4. **An American Dream** (*Express*)
5. **If There's a Heaven Above** (*Seventh Dream of a Teenage Heaven*)
6. **So Alive** (*Love and Rockets*)
7. **Kundalini Express** (*Express*)
8. **No Big Deal** (*Love and Rockets*)
9. **The Dog-End of A Day Gone By** (*Seventh Dream of a Teenage Heaven*)
10. **Yin and Yang and The Flowerpot Men** (*Express*)
11. **Mirror People** (*Earth, Sun, Moon*)

Fun Fact: Love and Rockets got their name from the comic book of the same name.

Song Note (So Alive): The song is about a girl that singer/guitarist Daniel Ash saw at a party and was instantly infatuated with, even though he was recently married. "So Alive" is how the girl made him feel.

157

MADNESS

Before video games overtook us with their addictive problem-solving, we yearned for something to challenge our brains. TV shows like *Happy Days*, *Love Boat* and *Dukes of Hazzard* weren't the intellectual stimulation we craved. Straight outta Hungary came a puzzle game called the Rubik's Cube. The Rubik's Cube had nine squares per side, each side being a different color. You could rotate the squares mixing up the colors. The goal was to unmix the squares to get the colors back on the same side. In second grade, a classmate brought in one for show and tell. The mixed-up Rubik's Cube was passed around the class, but no one could solve it. It was *maddening*. Then it came to me. I immediately noticed that the colors on the cube were just stickers. Secretly, I moved the stickers to the correct sides, solving it. Did I cheat or did I pull a Kobayashi Maru? I didn't care; in second grade, it made me the class hero.

Despite their name, Madness was a fast-paced, vibrant, dance explosion. In a time of economic struggle, Madness' music spoke to the British working class, who needed an escape from the dull routine of their dismal lives. The band's brand of ska (2 Tone) became the light in a grey haze that hung over Britain's suburbs. In this time of social strife, instead of splitting the colors of society, Madness encouraged mixing it up. Drawing on musical influences from many ethnic genres, such as reggae and calypso, Madness became a unifying force in divisive times.

Albums of the '80s:

Absolutely (1980)
Work Rest And Play (1980)
7 (1981)
The Rise And Fall (1982)
Keep Moving (1984)
Mad Not Mad (1985)
The Madness (1988)

The 11 Best Songs By Madness:

1. **Embarrassment** (*Absolutely*)
2. **Disappear** (*Absolutely*)
3. **Sign of the Times** (*7*)
4. **Our House** (*The Rise and Fall*)
5. **Song In Red** (*The Madness*)
6. **Shut Up** (*7*)
7. **On The Beat Pete** (*Absolutely*)
8. **Samantha** (*Keep Moving*)
9. **Mrs. Hutchinson** (*7*)
10. **The Sun And Rain** (*Keep Moving*)
11. **It Must Be Love** (*7*)

Fun Fact: In 1981, the band made a scripted movie about their beginnings and rise to fame called "Take It Or Leave It." The film starred the members of the band playing themselves.

MADONNA

Florence Griffith Joyner was one of the fastest women of all time. She was faster than a speeding bullet. If she delivered pizzas for Domino's, you would get your pizza before you ordered it. Flo-Jo ran so fast, I bet she had more speeding tickets than race car driver, Rick Mears. She was a superhuman icon, whose speed carried her to win three gold medals in the 1988 Olympics, breaking world records like Ricky Schroeder broke hearts. In a decade that was thin on female role models, Flo-Jo raced to the top as a hero for many little girls.

Madonna ruled pop radio in the '80s. She had a bold, charismatic, earth-shaking, glass-ceiling-shattering voice unlike any we've ever witnessed. Madonna may have debuted with a candy-coated girl next door image, but with each subsequent release, she peeled back the layers of the female stereotype, challenging societal norms and expressing herself in ways we never expected. Many critics called her a controversial bad girl, but while her lyrics were controversial to a mainstream audience, Madonna sang about subjects that women faced on a daily basis. When she sang about teen pregnancy, abusive fathers, parental deceit, and religious hypocrisy, she was singing to women in a grounded way, letting them know that they are not alone facing struggles that many people didn't want to admit existed. In a decade short on superhero films, Madonna was a wonder for women everywhere.

Albums of the '80s:

Madonna (1983)
Like A Virgin (1984)
True Blue (1986)
Like A Prayer (1989)

The 11 Best Non-Single Madonna Songs:

It would be easy to list Madonna's radio hits. Instead, I wanted to shine a light on the overlooked songs in her catalog. All songs below were never officially released as singles.

1. **Stay** (*Like A Virgin*)
2. **Til Death Do Us Part** (*Like A Prayer*)
3. **Physical Attraction** (*Madonna*)
4. **Love Song** (*Like A Prayer*)
5. **Love Makes The World Go Round** (*True Blue*)
6. **Love Don't Live Here Anymore** (*Like A Virgin*)
7. **Promise To Try** (*Like A Prayer*)
8. **Pretender** (*Like A Prayer*)
9. **Think of Me** (*Madonna*)
10. **Where's The Party** (*True Blue*)
11. **Supernatural** (*Cherish* Single)

Fun Fact: Madonna has a huge family. Her father was Italian, and her mother was French-Canadian. Madonna Louise Ciccione has three brothers and two sisters along with one half-brother and one half-sister.

MEGADETH

At midnight on Friday nights, MTV used to have a show dedicated to guys who didn't have anything to do. It was called *Headbanger's Ball* and featured videos from the most audacious metal bands on the planet. Whether it was Guns N' Roses welcoming us to their jungle or Mötley Crüe kick-starting your heart, *Headbanger's Ball* was the first to play it. It wasn't just the prettiest bands who came to the ball. Sure, they had the Cinderellas, the Faster Pussycats, and the Vixens; but The Ball dove deep in the underbelly of metal, flushing out the ugliest bands that had ever bitten the head off a bat. From the full speed attack of Anthrax and Pantera to the growling intensity of Overkill and Sacred Reich to the medieval madness of King Diamond, they all shared the spotlight. This is where I first saw Megadeth.

In the "Wake Up" video, lead singer Dave Mustaine tore through his guitar solo like his soul was on fire while crazed fans crawled all over a metal cage like rabid worms. It was more intense than a watching a group of teenagers get their heads lopped off by a man in a hockey mask. Dave Mustaine looked like there was something seriously wrong with him; that he had unbridled evil lurking in his heart. Maybe Dave harbored a lot of bitterness over being kicked out of Metallica. Maybe he's sold his soul to George Burns. Whatever the reason for his ferocious anger, the fans reaped the benefits. Metallica may have been the face of metal, but Megadeth has always been metal's emotional core.

Albums of the '80s:

Killing Is My Business...and Business Is Good (1985)
Peace Sells...But Who's Buying? (1986)
So Far, So Good...So What? (1988)

The 11 Best Songs By Megadeth:

1. **Peace Sells** (*Peace Sells...But Who's Buying?*)
2. **In My Darkest Hour** (*So Far, So Good...So What?*)
3. **Looking Down The Cross** (*Killing Is My Business...and Business Is Good*)
4. **My Last Words** (*Peace Sells...But Who's Buying?*)
5. **Mechanix** (*Killing Is My Business...and Business Is Good*)
6. **The Conjuring** (*Peace Sells...But Who's Buying?*)
7. **Wake Up Dead** (*Peace Sells...But Who's Buying?*)
8. **Rattlehead** (*Killing Is My Business...and Business Is Good*)
9. **Devil's Island** (*Peace Sells...But Who's Buying?*)
10. **Killing Is My Business...and Business Is Good** (*Killing Is My Business...and Business Is Good*)
11. **Set The World Afire** (*So Far, So Good...So What?*)

Fun Fact: After getting an advance from their record label to record their debut album, the band burned through the money, spending it on food, drugs, and alcohol. Out of cash, the band fired their producer and recorded the album themselves.

MEN AT WORK

In my high school, students were allowed to leave campus for lunch. I didn't have a car, so I had to beg an upper-classman with wheels to take my friends and me to whatever fast food we were craving that day. Did we want to go to Taco Bell for their flour hard shell Taco Light? Did we want the McDLT from McDonald's or the Veal Parmigiana from Burger King? Wendy's had their signature salad bar but I've never known anyone to order it. The '80s had a lot of growing pains in the fast food sector. How else can you explain McDonald's selling pizza?

In Australia, McDonald's offers vegemite spread, a yeast-based sweet and salty condiment. Vegemite sandwiches (Australia's PB&J) are two pieces of bread with Vegemite spread. It was made internationally popular by the Australian band, Men At Work, who mentioned it in their song, "Down Under." Ironically, the song "Down Under," which is a protest song about the over-capitalization of Australia, has gone on to be the song featured in every advertisement for Australia. Men At Work's grassroots, rocking reggae vibe along with Colin Hay's country sounding voice made them instantly accessible to American audiences. Even though you wouldn't expect a band that specialized in flute jams to be commercially appealing, they were. The passionate emotion in Hay's lyrics added wit to their profound criticism of social inequalities.

Albums of the '80s:

Business As Usual (1981)
Cargo (1983)
Two Hearts (1985)

The 11 Best Songs By Men At Work:

1. **Who Can It Be Now?** (*Business As Usual*)
2. **Be Good Johnny** (*Business As Usual*)
3. **Overkill** (*Cargo*)
4. **Down Under** (*Business As Usual*)
5. **It's A Mistake** (*Cargo*)
6. **Man With Two Hearts** (*Two Hearts*)
7. **Helpless Automaton** (*Business As Usual*)
8. **No Restrictions** (*Cargo*)
9. **I Can See It In Your Eyes** (*Business As Usual*)
10. **Everything I Need** (*Two Hearts*)
11. **Crazy** (*Down Under Single*)

Fun Fact: The band's debut album spent 15 weeks at number one on the US charts and was finally knocked out of the top spot by Michael Jackson's *Thriller*.

Song Note (Who Can It Be Now?): Singer Colin Hay lived in an apartment next to drug dealers. Addicts constantly confused his apartment with the drug dealer's place. Hay was unnerved every time there was a knock at his front door, inspiring him to write the song.

METALLICA

In the vast cesspool of '80s metal bands, Metallica emerged as the most metal of them all. And in the action-packed movies of the '80s, James Cameron emerged as the best action director out there, and he did it with only two movies. These two movies (*Aliens* and *Terminator*) were so good that all the other action movies combined couldn't match them. *Aliens* was an XXL sequel with Sigourney Weaver as the most kick-ass woman to ever hold a pulse rifle. I was too young to buy a ticket for the movie, so I bought tickets to see *Club Paradise* then snuck into *Aliens*. I did that so many times; I'm sure half of Robin Williams' box office can be traced back to me. Cameron's other masterpiece is the *Terminator*. The Terminator is an unstoppable full-tilt metal robot sent from the future with one agenda: to seek and destroy. The Terminator was played by actor Arnold Schwarzenegger before he became the Governor of California (and we thought that was the oddest elected official we'd ever see). With Arnold's commanding performance, the Terminator became one of the most iconic movie characters of all time. The Terminator was an indestructible force. It could punch through walls; it could crush your skull with its hands. It was a raw, powerful machine that couldn't even be stopped by time. If the Terminator was a metal band, it would be Metallica. If the Terminator was a pop band, it would be Metallica. If the Terminator was a rapper, it would be Metallica. And...if Metallica was a Terminator, it would be Metallica.

Albums of the '80s:

Kill 'Em All (1983)
Ride The Lightning (1984)
Master of Puppets (1986)
The $5.98 EP: Garage Days Re-Revisited (1987)
...And Justice For All (1988)

The 11 Best Songs By Metallica:

1. **...And Justice For All** (*...And Justice For All*)
2. **One** (*...And Justice For All*)
3. **Fade To Black** (*Ride The Lightning*)
4. **Last Caress** (*Garage Days*)
5. **Four Horsemen** (*Kill 'Em All*)
6. **Master of Puppets** (*Master of Puppets*)
7. **Seek and Destroy** (*Kill 'Em All*)
8. **Blackened** (*...And Justice For All*)
9. **Sanitarium** (*Master of Puppets*)
10. **The Thing That Should Not Be** (*Master of Puppets*)
11. **Whiplash** (*Kill 'Em All*)

Fun Fact: Before they were a band, drummer, Lars Ulrich, placed an ad in the LA Recycler newspaper that read, "Drummer looking for other metal musicians to jam with Tygers of Pan Tang, Diamond Head and Iron Maiden." James Hetfield answered his ad.

MIDNIGHT OIL

Everything I know about Australia, I learned from watching Mel Gibson in the *Road Warrior*. In the film, there was a nuclear war and everything in Australia ended up looking pretty much the same as it did before the war. I learned that Australia has thousands of miles of highway with no rest stops. I learned the most popular jewelry item was spikes, unlike in America where it was Swatches. But like America, Australia did have cage match wrestling and Tina Turner. Before we realized that Gibson's onscreen crazy wasn't too far off from his real-life crazy, Mel was a heartthrob. This opened the door for other Australian heartthrobs like Hugh Jackman, Heath Ledger and Midnight Oil lead singer, Peter Garrett. That said, Midnight Oil would be better suited in the world of the *Road Warrior* than in the pages of the tabloids. Midnight Oil's music was a blistering scorched earth tirade about the corporate overlord's ravaging Australia's precious resources and trivializing the native tribes. They shouted dissertations against tyranny and screamed in defense of the rights of the Australian people. Just like Mel's character in the *Road Warrior*, who fought for the rights of the helpless, Midnight Oil became the flag carrying patrons of the voiceless. In the late '80s, Midnight Oil would finally bring their marching orders to America. Though they had been dominating the Australian airwaves for years, the states were finally ready for the rebellion. It wasn't just beds that were burning but an ignited passion for truth, justice, and the Australian g'day.

Albums of the '80s:

Bird Noises (1980)
Place Without A Postcard (1981)
10,9,8,7,6,5,4,3,2,1 (1982)
Red Sails in the Sunset (1984)
Species Deceases (1985)
Diesel and Dust (1987)

The 11 Best Songs By Midnight Oil:

1. **Hercules** (*Species Deceases*)
2. **The Dead Heart** (*Diesel and Dust*)
3. **Kosciusko** (*Red Sails in the Sunset*)
4. **Beds Are Burning** (*Diesel and Dust*)
5. **Dreamworld** (*Diesel and Dust*)
6. **If Ned Kelly Was King** (*Place Without A Postcard*)
7. **Somebody's Trying to Tell Me Something** (*10 to 1*)
8. **Sometimes** (*Diesel and Dust*)
9. **Written in the Heart** (*Place Without A Postcard*)
10. **Knife's Edge** (*Bird Noises*)
11. **Bullroarer** (*Diesel and Dust*)

Fun Fact: Lead singer, Peter Garrett, takes his political activism beyond the band and has been the President of the Australian Conservation Foundation and a member of the international board of Greenpeace. In the 2000s, he was elected to the Australian House of Representatives and following his term was appointed to be Australia's Minister of the Environment, Heritage and the Arts.

THE MINUTEMEN

I discovered the Minutemen when I discovered not everyone understands sarcasm. As a skater, I always thought I was tough. I wasn't. When my skate crew wasn't tackling garage-made ramps, we would hang out behind the mall and grind. Once, we were invaded by a group of hulking middle school kids. They probably weren't that hulking in retrospect, but any kid who had an extra couple inches on me was Andre The Giant. This roving band of outsiders brought their boombox, blasting the throbbing bass rumble of the Minutemen. The first question from the delinquents was a snarling, "Do you like the Minutemen?" I responded as any sarcastic person would, "They're okay, but I like the Secondmen better." I was immediately punched in the face. I hit back, but when 11-year-olds fight, it's one of the most pathetic things you'll ever see. There's a lot of upper arm flailing and plenty of misses. We both gave up but went on to brag as if we had won. What made the Minutemen stand out wasn't their ability to drive boys to pummel each other, it was their ability to fly their anti-establishment flag with such John Woo-like magnitude. The Minutemen's obtuse song structure with D. Boon's noodling guitar riffs and Mike Watt's ground-trembling bass had more in common with a free jazz excursion or a Grateful Dead jam than it did with the "loud and fast" ethos of the punk scene. With a potent core of ravaging fervor, the Minutemen would become one of the most influential bands on the '90s Seattle grunge scene. Not even the Secondmen can say that.

Albums of the '80s:

Paranoid Time EP (1980)
Joy EP (1981)
The Punchline (1981)
Bean-Spill EP (1982)
Buzz or Howl Under the Influence of Heat (1983)
What Makes A Man Start Fires? (1983)
Double Nickels On The Dime (1984)
Tour-Spiel (1984)
3-Way Time For Last (1985)
Project Mersh (1985)

The 11 Best Songs By The Minutemen:

1. **This Ain't No Picnic** (*Double Nickels On The Dime*)
2. **Political Song For Michael Jackson to Sing** (*Double Nickels On The Dime*)
3. **Life As A Rehearsal** (*What Makes A Man Start Fires?*)
4. **Shit From An Old Notebook** (*Double Nickels On The Dime*)
5. **If Reagan Played Disco** (*Bean Spill EP*)
6. **Search** (*The Punchline*)
7. **King of the Hill** (*Project: Mersh*)
8. **Sell or Be Sold** (*What Makes A Man Start Fires?*)
9. **Bob Dylan Wrote Protest Songs** (*What Makes A Man Start Fires?*)
10. **Black Sheep** (*Joy EP*)
11. **Take Our Test** (*Project: Mersh*)

Fun Fact: "Political Song For Michael Jackson to Sing" was written for Michael Jackson to sing. Mike Watt sent a copy to Jackson's management but never heard back.

MISSING PERSONS

In the '80s, we re-imagined what was possible. A brain surgeon took on aliens from the 8th dimension, a football quarterback traveled across the universe to face-off with Ming The Merciless, and a skinny kid from Reseda defeated the entire Cobra Kai army. We let our imaginations mold our reality. The '70s may have given birth to punk rock, but the '80s made it their own. The '80s took the genre of punk and drop-kicked it into a glossy, disco-infused, hyper-colored pool of keyboards. What emerged was the redefined version of punk, known as New Wave. New Wave enveloped the decade like an illuminated sports coat stolen from Max Headroom's personal wardrobe. New Wave had punk's passion but without punk's anger; it had disco's jubilation but with more lyrical humanity. New Wave was everywhere. It was Nic Cage's hair in *Valley Girl*; it was Martha Quinn's wardrobe; it was the eyeshadow around the eyes of Dale Bozzio, lead singer of the New Wave band, Missing Persons. Sparked by quick-witted lyrics and driving melodies, Dale's imp-like voice delicately serenaded our ears with visceral excursions through the seedy, yet, mesmerizing world of dark emotional alleys and alienating nightclubs. Dale's voice brought a cheery innocence to lyrics dripping in the grimy depravity of life. In a decade lost in superficiality, Missing Persons explored the darker themes that affected our human condition. Because of the band's candy-coated sound, you became enamored with the delinquency rather than repelled by it.

Albums of the '80s:

Missing Persons EP (1982)
Spring Session M (1982)
Rhyme & Reason (1984)
Color in Your Life (1986)

The 11 Best Songs By Missing Persons:

1. **Mental Hopscotch** (*Missing Persons EP*)
2. **Bad Streets** (*Spring Session M*)
3. **Walking In LA** (*Spring Session M*)
4. **Words** (*Spring Session M*)
5. **If Only For The Moment** (*Rhyme & Reason*)
6. **Color In Your Life** (*Color in Your Life*)
7. **Noticeable One** (*Spring Session M*)
8. **Windows** (*Spring Session M*)
9. **Destination Unknown** (*Spring Session M*)
10. **Surrender Your Heart** (*Rhyme & Reason*)
11. **The Closer That You Get** (*Rhyme & Reason*)

Fun Fact: Singer, Dale Bozzio (Consalvi), was a Playboy Bunny before she would meet her future husband Terry Bozzio at a recording studio for Frank Zappa. Terry Bozzio, Warren Cuccurullo, Patrick O'Hearn were all members of Frank Zappa's backing band before they formed Missing Persons with Dale.

MÖTLEY CRÜE

Metal ruled the '80s like an iron priest. It was dirty, nasty, loud and deliberately offensive in every way. And I'm just talking about the clothes. Metal music made an effort to push the buttons of good taste and the wife of future Vice President, Al Gore. His wife, Tipper Gore, led a group of disgruntled women against the violent and sexual lyrics in pop music that they deemed inappropriate for children. The Parents Music Resource Center (P.M.R.C.) created a list of the 15 most offensive songs. The list was known as the "Filthy Fifteen." On that vulgar song list was "Bastard," from the most inappropriate, obnoxious metal band to ever grind a mic stand, Mötley Crüe. Born out of the seedy back rooms of the Sunset Strip clubs and peeled off the broken heel of a leotard-wearing groupie came four of the grimiest, sleaziest, party villains who ever infested a Hollywood stage. The band was so raunchy it was like Sunset Blvd. chewed them up and spit them into the trash bin behind the Whiskey-A-Go-Go. The Crüe had such a vile reputation there wasn't a booth reserved for them at Canter's Deli like there was for other bands. For the Crüe, there was a security guard out front trying to keep them away. There wasn't a hotel room they didn't trash, a party they didn't crash, or a cheerleading squad they didn't ruin. They were every mother's nightmare and every teenager's idol. For the Crüe, it wasn't just about being the life of the party; it was about destroying every rule in existence on the way to making the most killer music to ever wear a leather jumpsuit.

Albums of the '80s:

Too Fast For Love (1981)
Shout At The Devil (1983)
Theater of Pain (1985)
Girls Girls Girls (1987)
Dr. Feelgood (1989)

The 11 Best Songs By Mötley Crüe:

1. **On With The Show** (*Too Fast For Love*)
2. **Too Young To Fall In Love** (*Shout at the Devil*)
3. **Live Wire** (*Too Fast For Love*)
4. **Looks That Kill** (*Shout at the Devil*)
5. **Wild Side** (*Girls, Girls, Girls*)
6. **Take Me To The Top** (*Too Fast For Love*)
7. **Kickstart My Heart** (*Dr. Feelgood*)
8. **Too Fast For Love** (*Too Fast For Love*)
9. **Shout At The Devil** (*Shout at the Devil*)
10. **Public Enemy #1** (*Too Fast For Love*)
11. **All In The Name Of...** (*Girls, Girls, Girls*)

Fun Fact: Mötley Crüe was the rock band that set the standard for rock bands being covered in tattoos. Very few other bands had tattoos when the Crüe started inking up. All four members are covered in tattoos with Tommy Lee topping well over 50 tattoos (though according to him, it's all one big piece of art). Not to be outdone, Vince Neil opened up his own tattoo shop in Las Vegas called "Vince Neil Ink."

MOTÖRHEAD

My family were avid skiers. We used to wake up at 6 a.m. and drive two hours to hit the slopes. We plowed through the morning ski runs like the steamroller in *Maximum Overdrive*. But, hitting the slopes in the sunny afternoon brought on such exhaustion, it was like trudging through the last few miles of a marathon without water stations. Then, came Jolt Cola. Jolt Cola was the superhero of cola. It had more sugar and caffeine than any other soda on the market. It was exactly as its name suggested; it jolted your system. Before Jolt, you would sleepwalk through the day. After Jolt, you could clean your room, do the laundry, wash the dishes, mow the lawn, go grocery shopping, run 10 miles and read an entire Tom Clancy book all while you were still drinking it. If you had a Jolt Cola with your lunch on a ski day, your afternoon went from a sluggish chore to a Speedy Gonzales impersonation.

Listening to Motörhead had the same effect. Motörhead wasn't just a metal band; they were a metal band that drank a powder keg of Jolt after eating Popeye's spinach. Their songs fired electric shocks into your brain, sending your body into fits of extreme headbanging. One Motörhead song could empower you to accomplish anything. But like Jolt, Motörhead never went mainstream. They were the band that was appreciated by the purists for not just being better than the rest of the metal bands but for being the glowing green Loc-Nar of heavy metal that illuminated the way.

Albums of the '80s:

Ace of Spades (1980)
Iron Fist (1982)
Another Perfect Day (1983)
No Remorse (1984)
Orgasmatron (1986)
Rock 'n' Roll (1987)

The 11 Best Songs By Motörhead:

1. **Ace of Spades** (*Ace of Spades*)
2. **Love Me Like A Reptile** (*Ace of Spades*)
3. **Doctor Rock** (*Orgasmatron*)
4. **Cradle To The Grave** (*Rock 'n' Roll*)
5. **Dirty Love** (*Ace of Spades Single*)
6. **Loser** (*Iron Fist*)
7. **The Chase Is Better Than The Catch** (*Ace of Spades*)
8. **Rock 'n' Roll** (*Rock 'n' Roll*)
9. **Bite The Bullet** (*Ace of Spades*)
10. **Eat The Rich** (*Rock 'n' Roll*)
11. **Locomotive** (*No Remorse*)

Fun Fact: Before he had his own band, lead singer/bassist, Lemmy Kilmister was a roadie for Jimi Hendrix and a road manager for Emerson, Lake, and Palmer.

Song Note (Ace of Spades): The song is about gambling and risks. The title of the song refers to the "Dead Man's Hand" in poker, which is the hand that Wild Bill Hickok famously had when he was killed.

MR. MISTER

I grew up in a town called Visalia, California. I spent my entire childhood there before I left to go to college. When I was a kid, it was a small town, but it doubled in size as I grew up. Since I've left, it has doubled in size again. It's weird to go home because it's not the same place I remember. As much as I miss what my hometown used to be, what I really miss is my childhood and the environment that made me the person I am today. There is one band that always brings me back to that feeling I had when I was a teenager: Mr. Mister. There is something cosmic about their music that whisks me back to the uncertainty of youth, where the future was this mysterious road laid out before you. With every song, there's an optimistic mystique of hope, where you truly believe that anything is possible. Mr. Mister is widely considered a one-hit wonder, even though they have *two* big hit singles: "Broken Wings" and "Kyrie." And truthfully, those two songs are not even their best songs. It is the reason why Mr. Mister has so much nostalgia for me when it comes to reminiscing about the '80s. It's not just one or two songs, but it's their entire catalog that invokes that feeling of my adolescence. The music is so all-encompassing that it doesn't just capture the '80s culture but the feeling of everyday life in the decade. The feeling of getting pizza after a game, the feeling of driving home from your after-school job, the feeling of a road trip to whereabouts unknown. A feeling that in the future, we won't need roads.

Albums of the '80s:

I Wear The Face (1984)
Welcome to The Real World (1985)
Go On... (1987)

The 11 Best Songs By Mr. Mister:

1. **Hunters of the Night** (*I Wear The Face*)
2. **Partners in Crime** (*I Wear The Face*)
3. **Broken Wings** (*Welcome to The Real World*)
4. **Control** (*Go On...*)
5. **Is It Love?** (*Welcome to The Real World*)
6. **I'll Let You Drive** (*I Wear The Face*)
7. **Kyrie** (*Welcome to The Real World*)
8. **Runaway** (*I Wear The Face*)
9. **Stand And Deliver** (*Go On...*)
10. **Welcome To The Real World** (*Welcome to The Real World*)
11. **Dust** (*Go On...*)

Fun Fact: Almost all of the songs by Mr. Mister are co-written by John Lang, who was not a member of the band. Lang wrote a majority of the band's lyrics. When writing one of the band's biggest hits, "Broken Wings," he was inspired by the book *The Broken Wings* by Lebanese poet Kahlil Gibran. Gibran also had a big influence on the Beatles.

∏EW ORDER

In high school, New Order was my favorite band. There wasn't a day that went by where I didn't listen to *Brotherhood*, *Low-Life* or *Technique*. I always had a Walkman in my backpack so I could listen to the albums anywhere. My favorite New Order album was the second half of *Substance*. *Substance* was New Order's compilation of singles with a second disc of B-sides. But on cassette, the second album had a different collection of songs, which could only be purchased internationally. My parents took us on a trip to Toronto when I was in high school, where I was lucky enough to score a copy of the album. It had a song called "True Dub Faith" that was only available on this release. It was high school gold. When I brought it back to school, I was the envy of everyone on campus (well, really I was the envy of my circle of friends who liked New Order). Everyone asked me to lend it to them so they could do the '80s version of burning it and tape it for themselves. I refused every time. It was my prized possession. Until I folded. There was this girl. She was an upperclassman. Super cute and I could tell she liked me. She asked me with a crooked smile if I could loan it to her for the weekend. I said yes, fumbling it out of my backpack with all thumbs. She took it with the biggest grin, a hug and a kiss on the cheek. I never saw that cassette again. And I never got farther with the girl than that cheek kiss. Lesson to be learned: never lend your rare import New Order cassettes to cute girls...not even for the perfect kiss.

Albums of the '80s:

Movement (1981)
Power, Corruption, & Lies (1983)
Low-Life (1985)
Brotherhood (1986)
Substance (1987)
Technique (1989)

The 11 Best Songs By New Order:

1. **Sub-Culture** (*Low-Life*)
2. **True Faith** (*Substance*)
3. **Broken Promise** (*Brotherhood*)
4. **Love Vigilantes** (*Low-Life*)
5. **The Perfect Kiss** (*Low-Life*)
6. **Bizarre Love Triangle** (*Brotherhood*)
7. **Round & Round** (*Technique*)
8. **All The Way** (*Technique*)
9. **1963** (*Substance*)
10. **Paradise** (*Brotherhood*)
11. **Sooner Than You Think** (*Low-Life*)

Fun Fact: New Order's song "Blue Monday" is the biggest selling 12-inch single in the history of Britain. Because their label, Factory Records, was not part of the British Phonographic Industry Association, the single was not eligible to receive the notoriety or gold status that it earned.

STEVIE NICKS

The greatest story I know about Stevie Nicks is my favorite rock n' roll story, and actually it's not about Stevie Nicks at all. It's about Prince. When Nicks was recording her second solo album, *The Wild Heart*, she was listening to the radio when she heard Prince's song, "Little Red Corvette." She loved the underlying melody in the song and wanted something similar for a song she was writing. So, she called up Prince (because back then, rock stars just had each other's numbers when they wanted to chat). She said she loved his song and wanted his help with her new song. She sang him a bit of the lyrics. Prince took a couple of moments to percolate and finally said that he would be right over. Prince showed up to the recording location later that night. He jumped in the studio with Stevie and laid down the basic melody, playing the keyboards himself. After recording for a couple of hours, Prince bolted out of Nicks' life. He didn't even ask to take credit on the song for his contribution. The song that they recorded became Stevie's biggest solo hit, "Stand Back." Stevie Nicks wasn't a passing fad; she was one of the biggest female rock stars on the planet. Fleetwood Mac's *Rumors* was one of the best-selling albums of all time. You would think she didn't need anyone's help. But Stevie will be the first to admit that Prince's musical talent exceeded everyone. Nicks will always be as charming as she is gracious. Her positivity is contagious which is why her songs are so infectious. But even the best artists could always use a little Prince...

Albums of the '80s:

Bella Donna (1981)
The Wild Heart (1983)
Rock A Little (1985)
The Other Side Of The Mirror (1989)

The 11 Best Songs by Stevie Nicks:

1. **Stand Back** (*The Wild Heart*)
2. **Edge of Seventeen** (*Bella Donna*)
3. **Leather and Lace** (*Bella Donna*)
4. **I Can't Wait** (*Rock A Little*)
5. **Long Way To Go** (*The Other Side of the Mirror*)
6. **Sable on Blonde** (*The Wild Heart*)
7. **Nothing Ever Changes** (*The Wild Heart*)
8. **Stop Draggin' My Heart Around** (*Bella Donna*)
9. **No Spoken Word** (*Rock A Little*)
10. **How Still My Love** (*Bella Donna*)
11. **Talk To Me** (*Rock A Little*)

Fun Fact: Stevie Nicks originally planned to be an English teacher and was attending San Jose State University when she first started performing in a band. She was only one semester away from a degree when she dropped out to pursue her musical career.

Song Note (Stand Back): The keyboards on the song were written and played by Prince as an uncredited cameo.

OINGO BOINGO

It's Halloween night and you're headed to a party where no one's still alive. Gloomy music floats through the air as you enter a dark, cavernous room. You're surrounded by twenty-foot tall dancing skeletons, all illuminated brilliantly by that black light fluorescent glow. Mobs of people are screaming. A saxophone blares in the distance while an orange-hair banshee frolics across the main stage, jigging and jiving with a demonic sway. This isn't a haunted house with masked men looking to jump out and scare you to death; this was the annual Oingo Boingo Halloween concert which became a Los Angeles staple in the '80s. For the macabre fans of All Hallow's Eve, these concerts were a yearly pilgrimage. Oingo Boingo's Halloween shows weren't a scary farm fright fest; they were celebrations. A live Oingo Boingo show was a kinetic experience of electric energy. The music enveloped you like a blanket of youthful enthusiasm. It lifted your spirits rather than turning you into one. In fact, if you brought a dead person to one of the shows, there was a good chance that the music and atmosphere were so vibrant and powerful that the show could actually bring them back to life. It's not weird science, it's true, it happened to my ex-girlfriend; you can ask her, but she lives in Canada now. Oingo Boingo prided themselves on being a living, breathing party. A single moment at an Oingo Boingo show could make you feel young again, and that anything was possible. They weren't just good for your soul but good for young lads and little girls everywhere.

Albums of the '80s:

Only A Lad (1981)
Nothing To Fear (1982)
Good For Your Soul (1983)
So-Lo (1984)
Dead Man's Party (1985)
BOI-NGO (1987)

The 11 Best Songs By Oingo Boingo:

1. **Just Another Day** (*Dead Man's Party*)
2. **We Close Our Eyes** (*BOI-NGO*)
3. **Only A Lad** (*Only A Lad*)
4. **Private Life** (*Nothing To Fear*)
5. **Good For Your Soul** (*Good For Your Soul*)
6. **Weird Science** (*Dead Man's Party*)
7. **Stay** (*Dead Man's Party*)
8. **Not My Slave** (*BOI-NGO*)
9. **Goodbye Goodbye** (*Fast Times at Ridgemont High Soundtrack*)
10. **Who Do You Want To Be** (*Good For Your Soul*)
11. **Grey Matter** (*Nothing To Fear*)

Fun Fact: Though frontman Danny Elfman is known to be the heart and soul of Oingo Boingo, the band was originally started by his brother Richard as the Mystic Knights of the Oingo Boingo. When Richard moved onto filmmaking, Danny took the reins of the band and the creative direction. Coincidentally, Danny would also move over to filmmaking, scoring many big '80s movies like *Batman*, *Midnight Run*, and *Scrooged*.

ORCHESTRAL MANOEUVRES IN THE DARK

When discovering a new band, there are always various points of entry. Sometimes you hear a song on the radio, MTV, or from a friend. I began listening to O.M.D. through a greatest hits album. I'm not a fan of hits albums (ironic of me to say that). To me, greatest hits albums are just songs that were chosen by the record label to promote the band for radio play. Some songs on hits albums are truly great, but most of the time, the albums are loaded with filler singles that weren't hits. Bands evolve and change over time, so a lot of hits compilations are disjointed. Songs from a band's debut album don't always mesh well with songs 15-20 years into their career. It's like a teenager shopping for clothes with balding forty-year-old. Now, I wasn't unfamiliar with O.M.D., I had seen John Hughes movies. I was drawn to their song "Dreaming," which was only available on the greatest hits compilation. I had to purchase the entire album to get that one song. It's the '80s; it's what you did. O.M.D.'s music was like listening to an avant-garde electro-jazz band in an underground cafe on a space station on the planet Rylos. Though O.M.D.'s radio singles dripped with pop sentimentality, the rest of their catalog offered up dazzling songs stacked with intricate fusion of ideas. I would have never discovered their catalog without purchasing that compilation. Sometimes listening to the songs on the radio waves is the best maneuver.

Albums of the '80s:

Orchestral Manoeuvres in the Dark (1980)
Organisation (1980)
Architecture and Morality (1981)
Dazzle Ships (1983)
Junk Culture (1984)
Crush (1985)
The Pacific Age (1986)

The 11 Best Songs By O.M.D.:

1. **If You Leave** (*Pretty in Pink Soundtrack*)
2. **Enola Gay** (*Organisation*)
3. **Electricity** (*Orchestral Manoeuvres in the Dark*)
4. **Secret** (*Crush*)
5. **Tesla Girls** (*Junk Culture*)
6. **Dreaming** (*Best of O.M.D.*)
7. **So In Love** (*Crush*)
8. **Messages** (*Orchestral Manoeuvres in the Dark*)
9. **Souvenir** (*Architecture and Morality*)
10. **Joan Of Arc** (*Architecture and Morality*)
11. **Radio Waves** (*Dazzle Ships*)

Fun Fact: Originally, O.M.D. wrote the song "Goddess of Love" for the finale of *Pretty In Pink*. After they delivered the song, John Hughes changed the end of the movie and needed a new song by the next day. O.M.D. raced back to the studio, where they wrote and recorded "If You Leave" in one day. The rest is cinematic history.

THE OUTFIELD

Major League Baseball was America's #1 sport in the '80s. As a baseball card collecting kid, every year was filled with new heroes to root for. Opening a pack of trading cards was like Christmas. Were you going to get Fernandomania and the fiery arm of pitcher Fernando Valenzuela? Or would you get the exhilarating high of the NY Mets duo, Darryl Strawberry and Dwight "Doc" Gooden? If you were really lucky, you might end up with the most prolific hitting duo of the decade and get the Bash Brothers, Jose Canseco and Mark McGuire. In a desperate quest to get a rookie McGuire, I once traded a rookie Wally Joyner, Walt Weiss, and Will Clark to get a McGuire in near mint condition, which for McGuire was easy to bulk up to get back to mint.

Baseball even had its influence in England. One band was such a fan; they called themselves the Baseball Boys, which they later changed up to The Outfield. Though The Outfield was a British band, they struck out in their home country and became a hard hitter in the US. It's not surprising that their bang-bang style slid into the zone with American culture. Their carefree sound stole American hearts with a grand slam. The Outfield had a packed bullpen of great songs, but they ultimately will be remembered as a one-hit wonder for "Your Love." Like Kirk Gibson in the bottom of the ninth in Game One of the 1988 World Series, being remembered for one hit isn't a bad thing as long as it's the game-winning one.

Albums of the '80s:

Play Deep (1985)
Bangin' (1987)
Voices of Babylon (1989)

The 11 Best Songs By The Outfield:

1. **Your Love** (*Play Deep*)
2. **Playground** (*Bangin'*)
3. **All The Love** (*Play Deep*)
4. **61 Seconds** (*Play Deep*)
5. **Since You Been Gone** (*Bangin'*)
6. **My Paradise** (*Voices of Babylon*)
7. **Say It Isn't So** (*Play Deep*)
8. **Taking My Chances** (*Play Deep*)
9. **Somewhere In America** (*Bangin'*)
10. **Voices of Babylon** (*Voices of Babylon*)
11. **No Point** (*Voices of Babylon*)

Fun Fact: The song "Your Love" has stayed popular since its release and has had a considerable impact on other artists. There are over 1,000 covers of the song by other artists online.

Song Note (Your Love): The song is about a guy trying to convince his ex-girlfriend to have a one-night stand.

PET SHOP BOYS

I first heard the Pet Shop Boys song, "West End Girls," in Licorice Pizza while flipping through the record racks. I liked the song, immediately. My friend who was with me said that "West End Girls" was the weakest song on the album. If that was the worst song, I had to hear the rest. "West End Girls" is not a bad song, it was just very different than what the Pet Shop Boys would ultimately be more appreciated for, their dance music. The Pet Shop Boys became a band that had two different faces for two different audiences. They had their mainstream audience that devoured their radio-friendly emotive pop while club-goers begged for their dancehall anthems. The Pet Shop Boys were an '80s club staple, which they embraced. Immediately after the release of their debut album, they released a remix album (called *Disco*) that featured songs from their debut album that were amped up for club action. What they did was genius. Many bands would complain that they're tired of making music to appease a mass audience; they just want to make the music they want to make. Pet Shop Boys found a way to do both. By opening themselves to creating music that could be appreciated on all fronts, they opened themselves to new opportunities, finding new fans in new places they never imagined. They used their brains and their brawns to find the opportunities that would lead to their success. At least that's my impression of what they've done to deserve it.

Albums of the '80s:

Please (1986)
Actually (1987)
Introspective (1988)
Alternative (1989)

The 11 Best Songs By The Pet Shop Boys:

1. **Opportunities** (*Please*)
2. **It's A Sin** (*Actually*)
3. **Suburbia** (*Please*)
4. **Always On My Mind** (*Introspective*)
5. **I Want A Lover** (*Please*)
6. **Love Comes Quickly** (*Please*)
7. **That's My Impression** (*Alternative*)
8. **What Have I Done To Deserve This?** (*Actually*)
9. **Tonight Is Forever** (*Please*)
10. **Rent** (*Actually*)
11. **West End Girls** (*Please*)

Fun Fact: Neil Tennant of the Pet Shop Boys began his professional career working as an editor for Marvel comics.

Song Note (West End Girls): The song was inspired by the song "The Message" by Grandmaster Flash & The Furious Five, and it loosely borrows the drum beat pattern from Michael Jackson's "Billie Jean."

Set Break/111 Best Metal Songs of the Decade

I know metal music better than I know the names of the members of my family. The difficult journey in making this list was figuring out what bands belonged. Should this be a glam metal list or a hardcore metal list? What should I include? Hard Rock? Ballads? This is what I decided. Since this is a book about the '80s, I want my readers to know what it was like to hear these songs in the '80s. This list is the 111 best songs that you would hear on a metal radio station during the '80s. If you were alive in the '80s, were driving to the mall in your Buick Skylark and you flipped on the radio, this a list of the best songs you might hear. So get out your Aqua Net, polish off your combat boots and let's get ready to rock!!!

Here are the 111 Best Metal Songs:

1. **Shook Me All Night Long** - AC/DC (*Back in Black*)
2. **Panama** - Van Halen (*1984*)
3. **Paradise City** - Guns N' Roses (*Appetite For Destruction*)
4. **Livin' On a Prayer** - Bon Jovi (*Slippery When Wet*)
5. **Here I Go Again** - Whitesnake (*Whitesnake*)
6. **Unchained** - Van Halen (*Fair Warning*)
7. **Crazy Train** - Ozzy Osbourne (*Blizzard of Ozz*)
8. **Sweet Child O' Mine** - Guns N' Roses (*Appetite For Destruction*)
9. **Rock You Like A Hurricane** - Scorpions (*Love At First Sting*)

10. **Round and Round** - Ratt (*Out of the Cellar*)
11. **Live Wire** - Mötley Crüe (*Too Fast For Love*)
12. **Back in Black** - AC/DC (*Back in Black*)
13. **Breaking the Law** - Judas Priest (*British Steel*)
14. **Rainbow in the Dark** - Dio (*Holy Diver*)
15. **Master of Puppets** - Metallica (*Master of Puppets*)
16. **Welcome to the Jungle** - Guns N' Roses (*Appetite For Destruction*)
17. **Photograph** - Def Leppard (*Pyromania*)
18. **Run To The Hills** - Iron Maiden (*Number of the Beast*)
19. **Gypsy Road** - Cinderella (*Long Cold Winter*)
20. **Cum On Feel The Noize** - Quiet Riot (*Metal Health*)
21. **Hot For Teacher** - Van Halen (*1984*)
22. **Youth Gone Wild** - Skid Row (*Skid Row*)
23. **Kiss Me Deadly** - Lita Ford (*Lita*)
24. **Ace of Spades** - Motörhead (*Ace of Spades*)
25. **Too Young To Fall In Love** - Mötley Crüe (*Shout At The Devil*)
26. **One** - Metallica (*...And Justice For All*)
27. **You've Got Another Thing Comin'** - Judas Priest (*Screaming For Vengeance*)
28. **Raining Blood** - Slayer (*Reign In Blood*)
29. **The Zoo** - Scorpions (*Animal Magnetism*)
30. **Scared** - Dangerous Toys (*Dangerous Toys*)
31. **Runaway** - Bon Jovi (*Bon Jovi*)
32. **Modern Day Cowboy** - Tesla (*Mechanical Resonance*)
33. **In My Dreams** - Dokken (*Under Lock And Key*)
34. **Give Me All Your Love** - Whitesnake (*Whitesnake*)
35. **Born To Be My Baby** - Bon Jovi (*New Jersey*)
36. **Rock Brigade** - Def Leppard (*On Through The Night*)
37. **No One Like You** - Scorpions (*Blackout*)
38. **Kickstart My Heart** - Mötley Crüe (*Dr. Feelgood*)
39. **Shake Me** - Cinderella (*Night Songs*)
40. **Rock Me** - Great White (*Once Bitten*)

41. **We're Not Gonna Take It** - Twisted Sister (*Stay Hungry*)
42. **Who Made Who** - AC/DC (*Who Made Who*)
43. **Is This Love?** - Whitesnake (*Whitesnake*)
44. **Never Enough** - LA Guns (*Cocked and Loaded*)
45. **House of Pain** - Faster Pussycat (*Wake Me When It's Over*)
46. **Eyes Of A Stranger** - Queensrÿche (*Operation: Mindcrime*)
47. **I Remember You** - Skid Row (*Skid Row*)
48. **You Give Love a Bad Name** - Bon Jovi (*Slippery When Wet*)
49. **Living After Midnight** - Judas Priest (*British Steel*)
50. **For Whom The Bell Tolls** - Metallica (*Ride The Lightning*)
51. **Don't Know What You Got (Till It's Gone)** - Cinderella (*Long Cold Winter*)
52. **18 and Life** - Skid Row (*Skid Row*)
53. **Peace Sells** - Megadeth (*Peace Sells... but Who's Buying?*)
54. **Mr. Crowley** - Ozzy Osbourne (*Blizzard of Ozz*)
55. **Metal Health (Bang Your Head)** - Quiet Riot (*Metal Health*)
56. **Can I Play With Madness** - Iron Maiden (*Seventh Son of a Seventh Son*)
57. **Love Bites** - Def Leppard (*Hysteria*)
58. **Still Loving You** - Scorpions (*Love At First Sting*)
59. **Fallen Angel** - Poison (*Open Up and Say...Ahh!*)
60. **Looks that Kill** - Mötley Crüe (*Shout At The Devil*)
61. **The Final Countdown** - Europe (*The Final Countdown*)
62. **Tragedy** - Hanoi Rocks (*Bangkok Shocks, Saigon Shakes, Hanoi Rocks*)

63. **Talk Dirty To Me** - Poison (*Look What The Cat Dragged In*)
64. **Paradise** - Tesla (*The Great Radio Controversy*)
65. **Pour Some Sugar On Me** - Def Leppard (*Hysteria*)
66. **Edge of A Broken Heart** - Vixen (*Vixen*)
67. **Somebody Save Me** - Cinderella (*Night Songs*)
68. **Someone Like You** - Bang Tango (*Psycho Cafe*)
69. **Little Fighter** - White Lion (*Big Game*)
70. **Holy Diver** - Dio (*Holy Diver*)
71. **Too Fast For Love** - Mötley Crüe (*Too Fast For Love*)
72. **Love Song** - Tesla (*The Great Radio Controversy*)
73. **Big City Nights** - The Scorpions (*Love At First Sting*)
74. **Bringing On the Heartbreak** - Def Leppard (*High 'N' Dry*)
75. **Only Lonely** - Bon Jovi (*7800 Fahrenheit*)
76. **Still of the Night** - Whitesnake (*Whitesnake*)
77. **Jump** - Van Halen (*1984*)
78. **Hang Tough** - Tesla (*The Great Radio Controversy*)
79. **I Wanna Rock** - Twisted Sister (*Stay Hungry*)
80. **Shout At The Devil** - Mötley Crüe (*Shout At the Devil*)
81. **Alone Again** - Dokken (*Tooth and Nail*)
82. **Wait** - White Lion (*Pride*)
83. **Nobody's Fool** - Cinderella (*Night Songs*)
84. **Breaking the Chains** - Dokken (*Breaking The Chains*)
85. **Dreams** - Van Halen (*5150*)
86. **Heaven** - Warrant (*Dirty Rotten Filthy Stinking Rich*)
87. **Mirror Mirror** - Don Dokken (*Up From The Ashes*)
88. **Mother** - Danzig (*Danzig*)
89. **Smoking in the Boys Room** - Mötley Crüe (*Theatre of Pain*)
90. **Once Bitten, Twice Shy** - Great White (*...Twice Shy*)
91. **Princess of the Night** - Saxon (*Denim and Leather*)
92. **Metal on Metal** - Anvil (*Metal on Metal*)
93. **Madalaine** - LA Guns (*Cocked and Loaded*)

94. **Under the Gun** - Danger Danger (*Danger Danger*)
95. **Home Sweet Home** - Mötley Crüe (*Theatre of Pain*)
96. **Armageddon It** - Def Leppard (*Hysteria*)
97. **Wanted Dead Or Alive** - Bon Jovi (*Slippery When Wet*)
98. **Mean Street** - Van Halen (*Fair Warning*)
99. **I Love It Loud** - Kiss (*Creatures of the Night*)
100. **Coming Home** - Cinderella (*Long Cold Winter*)
101. **Standing on the Outside** - Dokken (*Lightning Strikes Again*)
102. **Wanted Man** - Ratt (*Out of the Cellar*)
103. **Animal** - Def Leppard (*Hysteria*)
104. **Dr. Feelgood** - Mötley Crüe (*Dr. Feelgood*)
105. **Lay Your Hands On Me** - Bon Jovi (*New Jersey*)
106. **Screaming Blue Murder** - Girlschool (*Screaming Blue Murder*)
107. **Mama Weer All Crazee Now** - Quiet Riot (*Condition Critical*)
108. **Close My Eyes Forever** - Lita Ford/Ozzy Osbourne (*Lita*)
109. **Summertime Girls** - Y&T (*Down for the Count*)
110. **Rock You To Hell** - Grim Reaper (*Rock You To Hell*)
111. **I Wanna Be Somebody** - W.A.S.P. (*W.A.S.P.*)

TOM PETTY AND THE HEARTBREAKERS

In the '70s, Tom Petty strutted out of the Florida swamps and kicked us in the eardrums with pure rock n' roll. In the '90s, Petty had a massive rebirth ignited by his iconic solo album, *Full Moon Fever*. But in between the '70s and the '90s, Petty took the road less traveled. The '80s may be Petty's most subversive decade. The decade was owned by MTV. Petty couldn't dance like Michael Jackson and he couldn't wear a dress like Madonna. He couldn't rap like LL Cool J and claymation just wasn't his thing. But Petty and the boys were churning out music that stood on par with the best of their career.

Narrowing Petty's '80s career down to eleven songs isn't just a difficult task... it's an insult. Petty is one of the greats. Time and time again he has stood up to the record companies and won. He is everything that rock n' roll was and everything it should be. He has stood for artists' rights. He has stood against over-production. He blasted the radio industry, *American Idol*, and the record labels for every wrong turn they've taken. He made a 4-hour music documentary, which happens to be one of the greatest music documentaries of all time. No matter how much Petty stands for or stands against, he backs it up making good honest music that only gets better with time.

Rock on, Tom Petty. Rock on forever.

Albums of the '80s:

Hard Promises (1981)

Long After Dark (1982)

Southern Accents (1985)

Let Me Up (I've Had Enough) (1987)

The 11 Best Songs By
Tom Petty And The Heartbreakers:

1. **A Woman In Love (It's Not Me)** *(Hard Promises)*
2. **Change Of Heart** *(Long After Dark)*
3. **Rebels** *(Southern Accents)*
4. **The Waiting** *(Hard Promises)*
5. **Don't Come Around Here No More** *(Southern Accents)*
6. **Deliver Me** *(Long After Dark)*
7. **Insider** *(Hard Promises)*
8. **Runaway Trains** *(Let Me Up I've Had Enough)*
9. **You Got Lucky** *(Long After Dark)*
10. **We Stand A Chance** *(Long After Dark)*
11. **Jammin' Me** *(Let Me Up I've Had Enough)*

Fun Fact: Petty's record label (MCA) wanted to release *Hard Promises* for $9.98 instead of $8.98. In protest, Petty said he would re-name the album $8.98 if they did. Petty won and the label kept the album at the $8.98 sales price.

THE POLICE

My brother used to be obsessed with the Police. He'd listen to the band on repeat behind closed doors. We had thin walls in our house, so by default, I quickly learned every Police song by heart whether I wanted to or not. There would be times when I'd start humming Quiet Riot's "Mama Weer All Crazee Now" only to end up humming "Don't Stand So Close To Me" and I would have no idea how I got there. (Yes, I used to listen to Quiet Riot; let's just pretend it never happened and move on).

My brother was the self-proclaimed authority on the Police. He would walk around the house spouting random facts about the band; I don't know if any of them were accurate or if he was just building their hype. He once told me Sting proclaimed that musical artists only had five good albums in them. After those five albums, everything was crap. The Police did put out five high-quality albums before breaking up. I vaguely remember reading once in a magazine (∞) that Sting said the Police had reached the Mount Everest of their career so they had to break-up. Oddly, Sting didn't follow his rule when it came to his own solo career. Maybe he's still trying to make five good ones. At least he got a pretty nice Jaguar out of the deal.

(∞) **80s Note:** A magazine was a printed version of the internet.

Albums of the '80s:

Zenyatta Mondatta (1980)
Ghost In The Machine (1981)
Synchronicity (1983)

The 11 Best Songs By The Police:

1. **Synchronicity II** (*Synchronicity*)
2. **Spirits In The Material World** (*Ghost In The Machine*)
3. **Every Little Thing She Does Is Magic** (*Ghost In The Machine*)
4. **Every Breath You Take** (*Synchronicity*)
5. **Wrapped Around Your Finger** (*Synchronicity*)
6. **Don't Stand So Close to Me** (*Zenyatta Mondatta*)
7. **King Of Pain** (*Synchronicity*)
8. **Driven To Tears** (*Zenyatta Mondatta*)
9. **Omegaman** (*Ghost In The Machine*)
10. **Synchronicity I** (*Synchronicity*)
11. **Tea In The Sahara** (*Synchronicity*)

Fun Fact: Stewart Copeland's father was an agent for the CIA. Because of his father's profession, Stewart traveled the world, growing up mostly in Cairo and other parts of the Middle East.

Song Note (Driven To Tears): The song refers to people's apathy towards hunger throughout the world.

THE PRETENDERS

I have always looked back on the 80s with fondness, that there was something magical about that era. In truth, the 80s were a mess. There was mass famine in Africa, hundreds of students killed by the Chinese military in Tiananmen Square, the Exxon Valdez spilled 11 million gallons of oil into the ocean, and someone shot John Lennon. In America, Wall Street crashed, and unemployment and homelessness went up. We endured, and we became stronger because of it. When we look back on the 80s, we focus on the moments when heroes overcame the limitations of the era. From the US hockey team's Miracle on Ice to the fall of the Berlin Wall, we celebrated achievement in the face of daily adversity.

The Pretenders faced more adversity than any band should ever have to. With two popular, critically-acclaimed albums, their future was bright. Then, Peter Farndon and James Honeyman-Scott both died from drug-related deaths within a year of each other. A tragedy like this would end most bands. But Chrissie Hynde soldiered on and re-assembled a new line-up. The band's third album, *Learning To Crawl*, became their best-selling album and spawned two of their biggest hits ("Middle of the Road" and "Back on The Chain Gang"). The upheaval continued as the Pretenders shuffled through six different guitarists in just the '80s alone. But the Pretenders are a shining example of rising above life's challenges and carrying on despite what it throws at you. The Pretenders are not pretenders... they are the real thing.

Albums of the '80s:

Pretenders (1980)
Pretenders II (1981)
Learning To Crawl (1984)
Get Close (1986)

The 11 Best Songs By The Pretenders:

1. **Mystery Achievement** (*Pretenders*)
2. **Middle of the Road** (*Learning To Crawl*)
3. **Talk of the Town** (*Pretenders II*)
4. **Brass In Pocket** (*Pretenders*)
5. **Message of Love** (*Pretenders II*)
6. **Hymn To Her** (*Get Close*)
7. **Kid** (*Pretenders*)
8. **Show Me** (*Learning To Crawl*)
9. **Pack It Up** (*Pretenders II*)
10. **The Wait** (*Pretenders*)
11. **Don't Get Me Wrong** (*Get Close*)

Fun Fact: Before Chrissie Hynde formed The Pretenders, she played in early versions of The Clash and The Damned.

Song Note (My City Was Gone): This B-side to the single "Back On The Chain Gang" went on to be the theme song for *The Rush Limbaugh Show*.

THE PSYCHEDELIC FURS

No one had a better finger on the pulse of the American teen culture than director, John Hughes. Hughes was so in tune with that world, when we think back on the '80s, it's John Hughes' vision of the world that we remember. Hughes had six iconic films that immortalized a generation: *The Breakfast Club, Some Kind of Wonderful, Ferris Bueller's Day Off, Sixteen Candles, Weird Science,* and *Pretty in Pink.* Every kid in America watched these films over and over until they were memorized. I guarantee you more kids in the '80s would recognize Anthony Michael Hall and Molly Ringwald than Ronald and Nancy Reagan. It wasn't just John Hughes films; it was all teen films. Did it have John Cusack in it? One or two Coreys? Was there time travel? We devoured them all: *Fast Times at Ridgemont High, Bill & Ted's Excellent Adventure, Summer School, Better Off Dead...* They spoke to us. They knew what we were feeling. These films didn't just define our world; they defined us. Most importantly, each film came with its own mixtape. The Psychedelic Furs' triumphant theme song to the film, *Pretty in Pink* was a beautiful addition to the soundtrack of our lives. The Furs weren't psychedelic; they were dreamers. Their songs were vivid dreams that wrapped you up like a pair of parachute pants. Even though Russia was going to nuke us out of existence, a great song still had the power to give us hope that there was a better place where Molly Ringwald was prom queen, and Jake Ryan was waiting outside by his car.

Albums of the '80s:

The Psychedelic Furs (1980)
Talk Talk Talk (1981)
Forever Now (1982)
Mirror Moves (1984)
Midnight To Midnight (1987)
Book of Days (1989)

The 11 Best Songs By The Psychedelic Furs:

1. **Love My Way** (*Forever Now*)
2. **Alice's House** (*Mirror Moves*)
3. **Pretty in Pink** (*Talk Talk Talk*)
4. **Heaven** (*Mirror Moves*)
5. **Into You Like A Train** (*Talk Talk Talk*)
6. **The Ghost In You** (*Mirror Moves*)
7. **House** (*Book of Days*)
8. **Heartbreak Beat** (*Midnight To Midnight*)
9. **Run and Run** (*Forever Now*)
10. **President Gas** (*Forever Now*)
11. **She Is Mine** (*Talk Talk Talk*)

Fun Fact: The Psychedelic Furs had songs on the soundtracks for the movies *Pretty in Pink* and *Valley Girl*. But Tim Butler of the band says their favorite film of the decade is John Carpenter's *The Thing*.

PUBLIC IMAGE LTD

Being a celebrity in the '80s had its perks. There wasn't a 24-hour news channel dedicated to what the stars of *Family Ties* were putting on their bagels that morning. There were not thousands of websites dedicated to every fashion faux pas Alyssa Milano made while pumping gas. There wasn't Twitter, Snapchat or whatever app was trending. If a celebrity died, you had to wait for the evening news or the morning paper to find out. Being a celebrity wasn't about the minutiae of their lives but about the quality of their art. Celebrities didn't have to worry about a misspelled tweet sidelining their career. To do something wrong, you had to do something really wrong. Just ask Pete Rose.

This was a perfect fit for John Lydon, singer of Public Image Ltd. Before P.I.L., Lydon sang for the punk rock pioneers, the Sex Pistols (when he was known as Johnny Rotten). By not being in the limelight all the time, and not having to worry about being in the limelight all the time, Lydon had the artistic freedom of not having to live up to a specific image. Instead, he managed to create a band that was a direct extension of his singing style. Neverminding the Pistols, P.I.L. was an eclectic blend of structure over chaos, introspection over anger, and artistry over rage. Anarchy continued to flow through Lydon's musical veins, using his lyrics as diatribes for everything wrong that crossed his path. For P.I.L., without constant expectations, their music was able to matter more than their public image.

Albums of the '80s:

The Flowers of Romance (1981)

This Is What You Want...This Is What You Get (1984)

Album (1986)

Happy? (1987)

9 (1989)

The 11 Best Songs By Public Image Ltd:

1. **This Is Not A Love Song** (*This Is What You Want...This Is What You Get*)
2. **Rise** (*Album*)
3. **Seattle** (*Happy?*)
4. **Like That** (*9*)
5. **FFF** (*Album*)
6. **Disappointed** (*9*)
7. **Home** (*Album*)
8. **Warrior** (*9*)
9. **Open and Revolving** (*Happy?*)
10. **Bad Life** (*This Is What You Want...This Is What You Get*)
11. **Fishing** (*Album*)

Fun Fact: After the Sex Pistols broke up, Virgin Records head, Richard Branson, flew John Lydon to Jamaica to meet with the band Devo. Branson was hoping that Devo would enlist Lydon as their new singer. Devo declined so Lydon created his own band, The Public Image with ex-Clash guitarist, Keith Levene. The band name would later be changed to Public Image, Ltd.

R.E.M.

In 1983, I first heard *Murmur* from my buddy's older sister when she locked herself in her room in a defiant act of teenage rebellion. We sat outside her door and listened to the album. As a youth, I thought "Radio Free Europe" meant the band was European, which is why they were so good. No American band could be this cool.

In 1984, I heard *Reckoning* when my babysitter and her boyfriend played "Pretty Persuasion" about 50 times in a row. I hated the song until college when I finally was able to listen to it again with some passion.

In 1986, *Life's Rich Pageant* was the soundtrack to junior high school. I listened to it on the way to school, when I got home, and in class. I memorized every song on the album so I could zone out when my teacher droned on about algebra.

In 1987, *Document* exploded onto MTV with the half-naked skater boy in the abandoned house. "It's the End of the World As We Know It" became the sing-a-long jam that everyone would attempt to sing but no one actually knew any of the lyrics past the first two lines.

In 1989, *Green* became a high school staple. I can't imagine a bus trip that didn't go by when I didn't throw the cassette into my Walkman and chill to "World Leader Pretend" or "I Remember California." The decade belonged to R.E.M. and would lead the way for them to dominate in the '90s.

Albums of the '80s:

Murmur (1983)

Reckoning (1984)

Fables of Reconstruction (1985)

Life's Rich Pageant (1986)

Document (1987)

Dead Letter Office (1987)

Green (1988)

The 11 Best Songs By R.E.M.:

1. **Pretty Persuasion** (*Reckoning*)
2. **These Days** (*Life's Rich Pageant*)
3. **Talk About The Passion** (*Murmur*)
4. **Harborcoat** (*Reckoning*)
5. **Orange Crush** (*Green*)
6. **The One I Love** (*Document*)
7. **Carnival of Sorts** (*Chronic Town*)
8. **Begin The Begin** (*Life's Rich Pageant*)
9. **So. Central Rain** (*Reckoning*)
10. **Pop Song 89** (*Green*)
11. **Driver 8** (*Fables of Reconstruction*)

Fun Fact: Michael Stipe (singer) met Peter Buck (guitarist) at a record store where Peter worked. They hit it off when they realized Michael was buying all the records that Peter had been saving for himself.

RED HOT CHILI PEPPERS

There is a divide between Red Hot Chili Pepper fans when it comes to their music. Old school fans only like the Chili Peppers from their debut album up to their '90s behemoth, *Blood Sugar Sex Magic*. Fans who discovered the Chili Peppers because of *Blood Sugar Sex Magic* think the Chili Peppers were at their best after that album. There is no dispute that there is a noticeable difference in the style of music before and after *Blood Sugar Sex Magic*. While both fans claim to be Chili Pepper purists, neither of them realize that the reason the Chili Peppers have survived the chaotic waters of the music industry is that they have changed to evolve. Of all the '80s bands that might survive 30 years into their career and would still be huge rock stars, no one predicted that the band who wore tube socks on their genitalia would reach that higher ground. The Chili Peppers weren't long shots because of their wild antics like playing naked, partying with River Phoenix or being strung upside-down by their feet on stage. The reason many people counted the Chili Peppers out was because in the '80s they didn't take themselves seriously. What the critics didn't realize was that even though their suits were too big and their underwear glowed in the dark, the Chili Peppers were classically trained musicians. They brought integrity to their music. Their songs were influenced by R&B, soul, funk, jazz, and blues. The Chili Peppers are proof that even if a band is made of serious musicians, having fun is a necessity to living long and prospering.

Albums of the '80s:

Red Hot Chili Peppers (1984)
Freaky Styley (1985)
Mother's Milk (1987)
The Uplift Mofo Party Plan (1989)

The 11 Best Songs By Red Hot Chili Peppers:

1. **Knock Me Down** (*Mother's Milk*)
2. **Taste The Pain** (*Mother's Milk*)
3. **Higher Ground** (*Mother's Milk*)
4. **Fight Like A Brave** (*The Uplift Mofo Party Plan*)
5. **Show Me Your Soul** (*Taste The Pain*)
6. **Johnny, Kick A Hole In The Sky** (*Mother's Milk*)
7. **Good Time Boys** (*Mother's Milk*)
8. **If You Want Me To Stay** (*Freaky Styley*)
9. **Nobody Weird Like Me** (*Mother's Milk*)
10. **Behind The Sun** (*The Uplift Mofo Party Plan*)
11. **True Men Don't Kill Coyotes** (*Red Hot Chili Peppers*)

Fun Fact: Flea grew up a trumpet player, with the goal of becoming a professional jazz musician, like his stepfather. He thought rock music was lame until his friend, Hillel Slovak, taught him how to play the bass. Flea was a trumpet prodigy as a kid, and his playing prowess can be heard on the album, *Nothing's Shocking* by Jane's Addiction.

211

THE REIVERS

I grew up in a small agricultural town, where the popular music was country. You couldn't walk into a store, a party or a restaurant without hearing about Dolly Parton's work hours or how Johnny Lee was still looking for love. Despite my exposure to it, I never connected with country music. Maybe it's because none of my exes lived in Texas or none of my heroes were cowboys. I was young; I wanted angry music. Country music was too positive to fulfill my sulky adolescent needs. But, whether I liked it or not, it became part of my DNA. I couldn't leave the country if I tried. When I first heard the Reivers, I couldn't believe I liked a band that sounded so country. The Reivers were part of the "New Sincerity" movement in Austin, Texas. These were bands, who infused country themes, twangs and melodies alongside indie rock lyrics and punk rock intensity. They were a country band *and* a rock band rolled into one. With jangly riffs that would make Michael Stipe smile and a southern drawl that would make Randy Travis say amen, forever and ever, the Reivers had that rebellious spark that thrived in me. Sadly, the Reivers never broke through commercially. They were country rock before country rock was cool. But they were one of the first to fuse country music and rock music, laying the foundation for bands, such as Uncle Tupelo, Ryan Adams, Calexico, Drive-By Truckers, My Morning Jacket, and Wilco.

Albums of the '80s:

Zeitgeist (1984)
Translate Slowly (1985)
Saturday (1987)
End of the Day (1989)

The 11 Best Songs By The Reivers:

1. **Truth To Tell** (*End of the Day*)
2. **Araby** (*Translate Slowly*)
3. **Jeanie** (*Saturday*)
4. **A Test** (*Saturday*)
5. **It's About Time** (*End of the Day*)
6. **End of the Day** (*End of the Day*)
7. **Baby** (*Saturday*)
8. **Wait For Time** (*Saturday*)
9. **Electra** (*Zeitgeist*)
10. **Legendary Man** (*Translate Slowly*)
11. **Once In Awhile** (*Saturday*)

Fun Fact: After the band's split, lead singer, John Croslin, went on to produce albums for Spoon and Guided By Voices.

Song Note (In Your Eyes): This is the only song that the band made a music video for. It was directed by Kevin Kerslake, who would go onto to direct some of the biggest videos of the '90s for bands such Smashing Pumpkins, Faith No More and Nirvana.

THE REPLACEMENTS

The Replacements were my first lesson in how bands change and evolve with time. In high school, I was on the swim team and I was pretty good. Unlike most sports, swimming involves a lot of sitting around waiting for your turn to compete. I would listen to songs before my races to motivate me. At one of our meets, I forgot to bring my Walkman. Luckily, I was able to borrow a friend's Walkman during the downtime. The Replacements' *Tim* was the only cassette he had. I pushed play. After getting doused by a scorching blast of energy from the song "Bastards of Young," I was grateful I had left my Walkman at home. The song was raw and relentless. I kept rewinding the tape and listening to it over and over. The song was the first song on side two, which made it easy to rewind. Trying to rewind to a song in the middle of a cassette was an '80s first world problem. After to listening to that song a bazillion times, I swam in my race and took first place. I told you I was fast.

A couple of years later, I picked up the Replacements album *Don't Tell A Soul*. It wasn't what I was expecting. It was different. It wasn't raw, rambunctious or wild. It was refined, produced, and glossy. I was annoyed. But I was a spoiled teenage brat. I expected every band to cater to my listening tastes. As I matured, I accepted that bands evolve; sometimes for better, sometimes for worse. Today, I love *Don't Tell A Soul* for its introspection and I have learned when a band evolves just let it be.

Albums of the '80s:

Sorry Ma, Forgot To Take Out The Trash (1981)

Stink (1982)

Hootenanny (1983)

Let It Be (1984)

Tim (1985)

Pleased to Meet Me (1987)

Don't Tell A Soul (1989)

The 11 Best Songs By The Replacements:

1. **Can't Hardly Wait** (*Tim*)
2. **Left of the Dial** (*Tim*)
3. **Alex Chilton** (*Pleased To Meet Me*)
4. **Bastards of Young** (*Tim*)
5. **I'll Be You** (*Don't Tell A Soul*)
6. **Black Diamond** (*Let It Be*)
7. **The Ledge** (*Pleased To Meet Me*)
8. **Sixteen Blue** (*Let It Be*)
9. **Here Comes A Regular** (*Tim*)
10. **Skyway** (*Pleased To Meet Me*)
11. **We'll Inherit The Earth** (*Don't Tell A Soul*)

Fun Fact: The band's first show took place at a halfway house for recovering alcoholics under their original name, The Impediments. The band was so bad; they were told they would never book another gig. Because of this, they had to change their name to find a place to let them play.

RUN-D.M.C.

In the early '80s, shoes were just shoes. You put them on your feet to protect you from the dangers of street life: nails, broken glass, used hypodermic needles (used hypodermic needles were everywhere back then). But in the middle of the decade, Nike changed the shoe game forever when they released the first basketball shoe named after a certain Chicago Bull, Michael Jordan. The shoe was called the Air Jordan, and it revolutionized footwear. America was Air Jordan crazy. Wearing a pair of Air Jordans was a status symbol on par with driving a Ferrari Testarossa or wearing a pastel suit. People fought over pairs, stole pairs, even killed for them. And for good reason. They were amazing. I adore Air Jordan shoes. When I wore my first pair, I fell in love. Real love. Not just one night stand love but the kind of love you remember forever. They were so comfortable and had so much support; I never knew my feet could feel so loved. Nikes weren't the only game in town. They had a rival: Adidas. Championing Adidas was the grandfather of all rap groups, Run-D.M.C. Run-D.M.C. burst out of the radio with confidence and bravado, spitting lyrics with such firepower you had to wear a helmet to protect yourself from the hard-hitting rhymes. They rapped with such strength you couldn't help but raise your fist in the air and fight for your right. They weren't a band; they were a force. They had their own style, their own wardrobe, their own walk, and their own shoes. Like Air Jordans, which changed the shoe game forever, Run-D.M.C. changed music forever.

Albums of the '80s:

Run-D.M.C. (1984)
King of Rock (1985)
Raising Hell (1986)
Tougher Than Leather (1988)

The 11 Best Songs By Run-D.M.C.:

1. **Rock Box** (*Run-D.M.C.*)
2. **It's Tricky** (*Raising Hell*)
3. **King of Rock** (*King of Rock*)
4. **Peter Piper** (*Raising Hell*)
5. **Run's House** (*Tougher Than Leather*)
6. **Walk this Way** (*Raising Hell*)
7. **It's Like That** (*Run-D.M.C.*)
8. **Mary, Mary** (*Tougher Than Leather*)
9. **Sucker M.C.s** (*Run-D.M.C.*)
10. **My Adidas** (*Raising Hell*)
11. **You Rock It Like This** (*King of Rock*)

Fun Fact: Joseph Simmons (stage name Run) is the younger brother of hip-hop mogul, Russell Simmons. Russell first brought Joseph in the business by getting him to DJ for rapper, Kurtis Blow.

Song Note (Rock Box): The video for the song was the first rap video to ever be played on MTV.

SHALAMAR

In 1982, Jeffrey Daniel and his band, Shalamar, were performing on *Top of the Pops*, when Daniel busted out a dance move called "the backslide." A year later, it would be re-named "the Moonwalk" when Michael Jackson performed it on the *Motown 25* TV special. Daniel, like his band, were major influencers in the world of R&B and dance.

R&B dominated the clubs with leg-trembling soul. The record label, SOLAR (Sounds of Los Angeles Records), shaped the urban dance scene. The label was co-founded by Don Cornelius, creator of *Soul Train*. If anyone knew dance, it was Cornelius. SOLAR had a roster of trendsetting acts, including the all-female powerhouse Klymaxx, the funky Midnight Star, the groove-intense Dynasty, the infectious boogie of The Whispers and The Deele, which featured Kenny "Babyface" Edmonds and Antonio "L.A." Reid.

The centerpiece of SOLAR was a group created by label co-founder, Dick Griffey, called Shalamar. The '80s iteration of Shalamar featured two soul train dancers, Jeffrey Daniel and Jody Watley, and vocalist, Howard Hewett. Following Shalamar's career is like tracing the blueprint of '80s R&B. From their disco-fueled beginnings to the funky distorted production to the wild jubilation of the new jack swing, Shalamar was a trailblazer whose music evolved before the times. Each album did more than just craft a new sound, they reinvented how we danced. Shalamar's music inspired and influenced artists in all genres, even today.

Albums of the '80s:

Three For Love (1980)
Go For It (1981)
Friends (1982)
The Look (1983)
Heartbreak (1984)
Circumstantial Evidence (1987)

The 11 Best Songs By Shalamar:

1. **Don't Try To Change Me** (*Friends*)
2. **Rocker** (*Go For It*)
3. **I Can Make You Feel Good** (*Friends*)
4. **You Won't Miss Love - Until It's Gone** (*The Look*)
5. **A Night To Remember** (*Friends*)
6. **Playing to Win** (*Friends*)
7. **Deceiver** (*Heartbreak*)
8. **Melody - An Erotic Affair** (*Heartbreak*)
9. **Make That Move** (*Three For Love*)
10. **Dead Giveaway** (*The Look*)
11. **Don't Get Stopped in Beverly Hills** (*Heartbreak*)

Fun Fact: Jeffrey Daniel was considered the master at a dance move called body-popping. Michael Jackson was a huge fan of Daniel and later hired him to choreograph the videos for "Bad" and "Smooth Criminal."

SIMPLE MINDS

In the '80s, there were five types of American teenagers: the athlete, the basket case, the brain, the criminal, and the princess. In every high school in the US, that's all that existed because all of those personalities existed in all of us. *The Breakfast Club's* cinematic achievement was being able to create five incredibly distinct characters that managed to embody traits that every teenager could relate to. These characters weren't just stereotypes; they represented a piece of our own personas. More importantly, as much as the archetypical American teen influenced John Hughes, John Hughes influenced the archetypical American teen. *The Breakfast Club* made us realize that our perception of our differences was a wall that prevented us from realizing how similar we all were. We became more accepting, more understanding, more aware. We realized that we no longer were individual fish swimming in a giant ocean alone, we were a united mass, facing the world together. As we grew into adults in the '90s, we brought forward a movement that re-shaped our world. It may be crazy to say that *The Breakfast Club* influenced our generation to bring about social and political change, it would be more ignorant to pretend that it didn't. John Hughes gave us an anthem, too. Simple Minds' "Don't You Forget About Me" was our battle cry. It was our fight song. It was an emotive outpouring of defiance. We were no longer the victims of the establishment but the champions of speaking out. Simple Minds, John Hughes and *The Breakfast Club* gave us our voice.

Albums of the '80s:

Empires and Dance (1980)
Sons and Fascination (1981)
Sister Feelings Call (1981)
New Gold Dream (81-82-83-84) (1982)
Sparkle In The Rain (1984)
Once Upon A Time (1985)
Street Fighting Years (1989)

The 11 Best Songs By The Simple Minds:

1. **Don't You (Forget About Me)** (*The Breakfast Club Sdtk*)
2. **Alive And Kicking** (*Once Upon A Time*)
3. **I Wish You Were Here** (*Once Upon A Time*)
4. **Someone, Somewhere In Summertime** (*New Gold Dream (81-82-83-84)*)
5. **Oh Jungleland** (*Once Upon A Time*)
6. **New Gold Dream** (*81-82-83-84*) (*New Gold Dream (81-82-83-84)*)
7. **Soul Crying Out** (*Street Fighting Years*)
8. **Hunter and The Hunted** (*New Gold Dream (81-82-83-84)*)
9. **Sanctify Yourself** (*Once Upon A Time*)
10. **Wonderful In Young Life** (*Sister Feelings Call*)
11. **Ghost Dancing** (*Once Upon A Time*)

Fun Fact: The Simple Minds usually write their own songs, but "Don't You Forget About Me" was written by Keith Forsey and Steven Schiff. Forsey co-wrote Irene Cara's Oscar-winning song, "Flashdance...Oh What A Feeling."

SISTERS OF MERCY

There was a radio station where I grew up that played underground alternative music after midnight on Fridays. As a young high school kid with limited access to new music, this exposure was a gift. Our town only had three music stores: a Sam Goody, a Musicland, and a Wherehouse. They were too busy promoting the new Wham! to stock bands like Sisters of Mercy. If I wanted to hear it, I had to be home from whatever high school party/dance/game/date in time for the show. This radio show was a portal to another dimension. When, I first heard the Goth epic, "This Corrosion," I was transported. Clocking in at 11 minutes, this was not a song I thought I'd hear on the radio. This was an operatic masterpiece. It opens with an explosive R&B tinged gospel howl that would make a clan of Benedictine monks chant. The song barrels forward with the power of a red Lamborghini speeding down a deserted suburban highway where dark clouds rain down Ian Curtis' tears. It culminates in a glorious "Hey now" sing-a-long like a zombie cheer squad competition finale. I was exhausted by the end of the song and I loved it. I immediately called my friend Elton (not John) to tell him. He already heard it. He said, "You think that's good, wait until you hear their song '1959'." I did. It was exhilarating. Sisters of Mercy will forever and always be looped in the goth genre, but they were more than that: they were rock, they were prog, they were gospel. They were their own musical dominion.

Albums of the '80s:

Alice (1983)
Reptile House (1984)
Body and Soul (1984)
First And Last And Always (1985)
Floodland (1987)

The 11 Best Songs By Sisters of Mercy:

1. **This Corrosion** (*Floodland*)
2. **Walk Away** (*First And Last And Always*)
3. **No Time To Cry** (*First And Last And Always*)
4. **Temple of Love** (*Temple of Love*)
5. **1959** (*Floodland*)
6. **Lucretia My Reflection** (*Floodland*)
7. **Dominion/Mother Russia** (*Floodland*)
8. **Alice** (*Alice*)
9. **Black Planet** (*First And Last And Always*)
10. **Flood II** (*Floodland*)
11. **Marian** (*First And Last And Always*)

Fun Fact: The band took its name from the Leonard Cohen song, "Sisters of Mercy." The band first heard the song in the Robert Altman movie *McCabe & Mrs. Miller*.

Song Note (This Corrosion): Singer Andrew Eldritch says the song is about the idiots who run around complaining about the corrosion and corruption in the world but are just as guilty as the forces they're pointing their finger at.

SKYY

Even though new wave, synth pop, and the new jack swing ruled most of the dance floors in the '80s, many people forget that at the beginning of the decade disco was still king. For the first few years of the decade, if you wanted shake your booty than you better be ready to come out with Diana Ross and get down on it with Kool and the Gang. You didn't need to be a super freak like Rick James or a bad girl like Donna Summer if you wanted to party in Funkytown. You just had to get so excited and the music would take you there.

I never thought in my angry youth that I would someday write a book with a disco band in it. In high school, if I was asked to listen to a disco song, it would invoke a punishment worse than having your butt cheeks duct taped together. But I've grown and I can't take full credit. It's rare for me to meet someone who has a similar musical knowledge that I have. One of my best friends from college gave me a run for my money. He was a huge early '80s R&B fan and taught me not to be close-minded when it came to music (even though I fought him on it). He opened my ears to a lot of new groups, new genres and new bands I never thought I'd enjoy. One of his favorite lesser-known groups was a band from New York called Skyy. What amazed me about Skyy was how every single song on their early '80s albums was a straight up solid dance jam. Their albums had no filler just pure dance floor exhilaration that made you wish the disco would never end. Sonny, thank you for the tunes. I'll miss you, buddy.

Albums of the '80s:

Skyyway (1980)
Skyyport (1980)
Skyyline (1981)
Skyyjammer (1982)
Skyylight (1983)
Innercity (1984)
From The Left Side (1986)
Start of a Romance (1989)

The 11 Best Songs By Skyy:

1. **Call Me** (*Skyyline*)
2. **Let's Celebrate** (*Skyyline*)
3. **Here's To You** (*Skyyport*)
4. **Music, Music** (*Skyyway*)
5. **Love Plane** (*Skyyway*)
6. **I Can't Get Enough** (*Skyyport*)
7. **Skyjammer** (*Skyjammer*)
8. **She's Gone** (*Skyylight*)
9. **Jam The Box** (*Skyyline*)
10. **Sendin' A Message** (*Start of A Romance*)
11. **Dancin' To Be Dancin'** (*Innercity*)

Fun Fact: Even though Skyy fell into relative obscurity in the middle of the '80s, after signing to Atlantic records, the band put out a big comeback album, ending the decade with a string of hits.

SLAYER

If it was true that hairspray from aerosol cans was the cause of the giant hole in the ozone layer, then the culprits behind this ecological disaster were definitely anyone involved in '80s glam metal. Back in the leather pants days of Hollywood's Sunset Strip, to be in the glam metal scene in any way, shape, or form meant that your hair had to match in every way, shape and form. Both women *and* men used dozens of cans of aerosol hairspray to project their hair as far into the air as possible. Their hair stood up so high that 747s had to divert their course to avoid a collision. Even Fletch's afro had hair envy. It was a necessity to make your hair harder than cement because when you were headbanging at the club the last thing you wanted was your hair to fall and end up looking like a member of A Flock of Seagulls.

Slayer is not hair metal. Slayer is the metal band that shits out hair metal bands. Slayer is the hardest of the hardcore. The thrashiest of the thrashers. Speed metal at its speediest. With Kerry King's titanic guitars riffs and Tony Araya's screeching vocals, the band tackled cuddly topics like mass killings, warfare, and everyone's favorite, the lord of darkness. Slayer was an experience, a lifestyle, a religion. Slayer fans are by far the most dedicated. They've endured countless controversies, from the many misinterpretations of the band's tongue-in-cheek lyrics. Yet, they still mosh through the pit with aggressive perfection. Because, if you don't understand Slayer's lyrics, then that's your fault.

Albums of the '80s:

Show No Mercy (1983)
Haunting the Chapel (1984)
Hell Awaits (1985)
Reign In Blood (1986)
South of Heaven (1988)

The 11 Best Songs By Slayer:

1. **Raining Blood** (*Reign In Blood*)
2. **Mandatory Suicide** (*South of Heaven*)
3. **Angel of Death** (*Reign In Blood*)
4. **The Antichrist** (*Show No Mercy*)
5. **Hell Awaits** (*Hell Awaits*)
6. **South of Heaven** (*South of Heaven*)
7. **Chemical Warfare** (*Haunting The Chapel*)
8. **Behind the Crooked Cross** (*South of Heaven*)
9. **Kill Again** (*Hell Awaits*)
10. **Dissident Aggressor** (*South of Heaven*)
11. **Aggressive Perfector** (*Haunting The Chapel*)

Song Note (Raining Blood): The song tells the story of a banished soul that comes back from Purgatory to seek vengeance.

Fun Fact: Guitarist Kerry King left Slayer to join Megadeth but quit after five shows. This created a rift and rivalry between Slayer and Megadeth that has never been fully resolved.

THE SMITHS

The first Smiths album I ever purchased was *Louder Than Bombs* on cassette. I had just received a new Walkman for graduating from junior high school, and I celebrated by purchasing a few albums. I don't remember the other albums I bought because the Smiths album was so incredible that it overshadowed any other album in my collection. My obsession with the album started from the very first listen. I went on an evening summer walk with my family and brought my Walkman with me because I was a moody teenager and being social with my parents was about the most uncool thing that could happen to me outside of a shake being poured on my head. The album was a patchwork of previously released singles and B-sides, but it beautifully flowed together like a blanket made of melancholy silk. There wasn't any other album in my collection at the time that was this consistently good. And it was a double album on top of that. It was 90 straight minutes of Morrissey's signature croon complimented by Johnny Marr's moody-enhancing melodies. The Smiths created a pool of emotional tidal waves that ensconced you like an endorphin-laced tsunami. Morrissey's voice fluttered with such romantic passion, it became a guiding beacon through the treacherous waters of jealousy, longing, and unrequited love. It was everything an emotional teenager can empathize with, even though they refuse to admit that they have any feelings. The Smiths were my confidant, my best friend, my Harry and my Sally.

Albums of the '80s:

The Smiths (1984)
Hatful of Hollow (1984)
Meat Is Murder (1985)
The Queen Is Dead (1986)
The World Won't Listen (1987)
Louder Than Bombs (1987)
Strangeways, Here We Come (1987)

The 11 Best Songs By The Smiths:

1. **There Is A Light That Never Goes Out** (*The Queen Is Dead*)
2. **Stop Me If You Think You've Heard This One Before** (*Strangeways, Here We Come*)
3. **Please Please Please Let Me Get What I Want** (*Louder Than Bombs*)
4. **Last Night I Dreamt That Somebody Love Me** (*Strangeways, Here We Come*)
5. **Still Ill** (*The Smiths*)
6. **How Soon Is Now?** (*Meat Is Murder*)
7. **Half A Person** (*Louder Than Bombs*)
8. **Panic** (*Louder Than Bombs*)
9. **I Want The One I Can't Have** (*Meat Is Murder*)
10. **Queen Is Dead** (*The Queen Is Dead*)
11. **The Night Has Opened My Eyes** (*Louder Than Bombs*)

Fun Fact: The Smiths picked their name because it was ordinary and they wanted ordinary people to have a voice.

SOFT CELL

Soft Cell is not a one-hit wonder, though they will likely always be labeled as one. The problem with Soft Cell trying to shed that image is that their song "Tainted Love" became a massive hit and eclipsed every other song they had in their library. There's another reason why "Tainted Love" prospered while many of their other songs didn't reach mass appeal; it was because of the R-rated content of their lyrics. The entire album, *Non-Stop Erotic Cabaret*, could be thrown on during the magic hour at some sweaty hole-in-the-wall Soho club where Mickey Rourke and Lisa Bonet are hanging out in a booth in the back. The title of the album perfectly describes the content. The songs on *Non-Stop Erotic Cabaret* are deviously sexual. They are erotic and profane. They may be explicitly sinister, but they are defiantly honest about the underground scene during the decade. Soft Cell lifted up the velvet ropes and pulled away the red curtain, revealing the underbelly of late nights after the clubs played their last song. Soft Cell wasn't trying to push boundaries; they were exposing the seedy truth of reality. They were the anti-pop pop band. Instead of the bubblegum pop of their predecessors, Soft Cell was the gum on the bottom of your shoe. They would stick with you into the next morning, proving difficult to scrape away, long after you left the club. Their songs found ways to embed themselves into your psyche, lingering for weeks at a time. They had an addictive catchiness that was enjoyable but still made you feel tainted for liking them as much as you did.

Albums of the '80s:

Non-Stop Erotic Cabaret (1981)
Non Stop Ecstatic Dancing (1982)
The Art of Falling Apart (1983)
This Last Night in Sodom (1984)

The 11 Best Songs By Soft Cell:

1. **Sex Dwarf** (*Non-Stop Erotic Cabaret*)
2. **Tainted Love** (*Non-Stop Erotic Cabaret*)
3. **Where Did Our Love Go?** (*Tainted Love B-Side*)
4. **Heat** (*The Art of Falling Apart*)
5. **Where Was Your Heart (When You Needed It)** (*This Last Night In Sodom*)
6. **Soul Inside** (*This Last Night In Sodom*)
7. **Insecure Me?** (*Non-Stop Ecstatic Dancing*)
8. **Mr. Self-Destruct** (*This Last Night In Sodom*)
9. **Chips on My Shoulder** (*Non-Stop Erotic Cabaret*)
10. **Bedsitter** (*Non-Stop Erotic Cabaret*)
11. **Martin** (*The Art of Falling Apart*)

Fun Fact: Donald Fagen of Steely Dan wrote and recorded songs with Soft Cell for their second album, but due to a label dispute, those songs were shelved. The band had to write and record *Non Stop Ecstatic Dancing* in one week.

Song Note (Tainted Love): Even though the song is a cover, Soft Cell's version has become the definitive version. There have been dozens of artists who have covered or sampled the song based on Soft Cell's rendition.

SPLIT EN2

In the '80s, if you wanted your video game fix, you had to dig through your couch cushions for quarters before heading down to your local arcade. Even as Atari and Intellivision emerged, they were still limited. Certain games could only be experienced in an arcade setting. Rapid-firing your fingers on *Track & Field* didn't have the same excitement on a joystick. *Centipede* was dull without its signature roller ball. And nothing came close to the wave of cartoon video games, like *Dragon's Lair* or *Space Ace*. I was in awe of cartoon games; I spent hours watching other players play. I had more enjoyment watching other players dump quarters into the machines than playing myself because once you saw the game completed, it lost its novelty. The fad quickly faded.

The New Zealand art rock band, Split Enz almost met with a similar fate. Though popular in their home country, audiences in Australia and the US were perplexed by their wild stage antics and their frenzied avant-garde sound. Faced with failure, the band shed their stage show spectacle and concentrated on making songs with substance. The results were international success. By weaving in elements of new wave without sounding harsh, and Beatles-esque melodies without sounding generic, the band adapted to the mainstream instead of stalling out by sticking to the safety of their comfort zone. If Dirk the Daring had expanded his range to something more than up, down, left, right, fire, then he might be around, too.

Albums of the '80s:

True Colors (1980)
Waiata/Corrobee (1981)
Time and Tide (1982)
Conflicting Emotions (1983)
See Ya' Round (1984)

The 11 Best Songs By The Split Enz:

1. **I Got You** (*True Colors*)
2. **One Step Ahead** (*Waiata/Corrobee*)
3. **History Never Repeats** (*Waiata/Corrobee*)
4. **Six Months In A Leaky Boat** (*Time and Tide*)
5. **Poor Boy** (*True Colors*)
6. **Message To My Girl** (*Conflicting Emotions*)
7. **Clumsy** (*Waiata/Corrobee*)
8. **Take A Walk** (*Time and Tide*)
9. **Breaking My Back** (*See Ya' Round*)
10. **One Mouth Is Fed** (*See Ya' Round*)
11. **What's The Matter With You** (*True Colors*)

Fun Fact: Brothers, Neil Finn and Tim Finn, are the two main singer/songwriters in Split Enz. After the band's break-up, the brothers would reunite and form a new band called Crowded House.

Song Note (I Got You): Neil Finn didn't like the chorus and always wanted to change it before releasing it. That never happened.

BRUCE SPRINGSTEEN

Whenever you go see your favorite artist in concert, you want a good show, especially because of the effort that you went through to get there. In the '80s, if you wanted to buy concert tickets, you couldn't log onto a computer to buy them, you had to find a store or ticket broker that was selling the tickets. If you wanted good seats, you had to get in line hours (sometimes days) before the tickets went on sale. Yes, for big shows, die-hard fans would wait in line *for days* just to buy tickets to see their favorite band perform. Now, if you waited in line for days to buy a ticket, the artist you were going to see had better make your effort worthwhile.

Of all the awesome live bands during the decade, one artist was boss: Bruce Springsteen and the E Street Band. Springsteen's concerts were the zenith of live rock n' roll. Their music was huge. It filled entire arenas like they were powered by a 100-piece orchestra while maintaining the intimacy and passion of a bar band playing their hearts out for free drinks. Springsteen concerts were marathons of serenading guitars that hit you like a wall of stampeding work boots. Forged in the blues-rock of the '70s, Springsteen knew how to put on a show no matter how long it took. Typical Springsteen shows lasted over three hours, making hard-working Americans late to work the next day every time they toured. Springsteen made it his goal to give every fan the time of their lives, so when they crawled into work the next day, completely exhausted, it was all worth it.

Albums of the '80s:

The River (1980)
Nebraska (1982)
Born In the USA (1984)
Tunnel of Love (1987)

The 11 Best Songs By Bruce Springsteen:

1. **The River** (*The River*)
2. **Dancing In The Dark** (*Born In The USA*)
3. **Atlantic City** (*Nebraska*)
4. **Cover Me** (*Born In The USA*)
5. **Nebraska** (*Nebraska*)
6. **Downbound Train** (*Born In The USA*)
7. **Brilliant Disguise** (*Tunnel of Love*)
8. **Hungry Heart** (*The River*)
9. **Two Hearts** (*The River*)
10. **Out In The Street** (*The River*)
11. **One Step Up** (*Tunnel of Love*)

Fun Fact: In the video for the song "Dancing in the Dark," Bruce pulls an eager fan out of the audience to dance with him on stage. Unknown at the time, it was actress Courtney Cox who would go on to play Monica Gellar on the massive hit '90s TV show, *Friends*.

Song Note (Hungry Heart): The song was originally written per the request of Joey Ramone of the Ramones. But the song was so good, Springsteen's manager convinced Bruce to keep it for himself.

THE SUGARHILL GANG

One of the cornerstones of hip-hop culture was (and still is) the fashion. Rap music and hip-hop fashion are so intertwined; there's an argument to be made: which came first, the style or the rhyme? The Sugarhill Gang is one of the first and one of the most important hip-hop groups of all time. Along with a handful of others, they ushered in an era of independence in a genre of music that was severely lacking in exposure. Like rap, hip-hop fashion was about bravado. It was about self-pride and promoting yourself. It was loud, in your face, and poetic. From clothes covered in brightly-colored, spray-painted graffiti to giant gold chains to larger than life sneakers sponsored by the world's greatest athletes, image was everything. What you wore defined who you were. Your clothes were your persona and, sometimes, they were more important than your personality.

In 1979, The Sugarhill Gang released "Rapper's Delight." It wasn't the first song to feature rapping, but it is the song that gave birth to an entire genre. In its 14 minutes of glory, it is the song that laid the foundation for every rap artist, song, and album that would follow it. The Sugarhill Gang would never have another hit that landed with that level of magnitude. So, everything that the Sugarhill Gang did after it tends to be overlooked and it shouldn't be. With potency and power, the Sugarhill Gang would continue to make game-changing, ground-breaking music that not only defined a decade but an entire genre.

Albums of the '80s:

The Sugarhill Gang (1980)
8th Wonder (1982)
Rappin' Down Town (1983)
Livin' In The Fast Lane (1984)

The 11 Best Songs By The Sugarhill Gang:

1. **Showdown** (*8th Wonder*)
2. **Hot Hot Summer Day** (*8th Wonder*)
3. **8th Wonder** (*8th Wonder*)
4. **I Like What You're Doing** (*Livin' In The Fast Lane*)
5. **Apache (Jump On It)** (*8th Wonder*)
6. **Kick It Live 9 to 5** (*Livin' In The Fast Lane*)
7. **On The Money** (*8th Wonder*)
8. **Sugarhill Groove** (*The Sugarhill Gang*)
9. **The Lover In You** (*Rappin' Down Town*)
10. **Rapper's Reprise (Jam, Jam)** (*The Sugarhill Gang*)
11. **Space Race** (*Livin' In The Fast Lane*)

Fun Fact: The Sugarhill Gang was assembled by Joey Robinson, vice president of promotions for Sugarhill Records. The label wanted to take advantage of the rap trend sweeping New York City, so instead of finding the best group, they opted to create their own rap crew. None of the rappers in the group are from New York. Wonder Mike, Big Bank Hank, and Master Gee are all from New Jersey.

TALK TALK

Every afternoon, my grandmother had the TV tuned to the scholarly white hair and saucer-sized eyeglasses of Phil Donahue. Donahue tackled important issues with fairness and toughness. His journalistic integrity and investigative diligence gave him the edge over daytime TV until the world was turned upside down by one woman: Oprah Winfrey. When Oprah's talk show debuted, it quickly rose to the top of the talk show ratings, even dominating Donahue. Oprah took on controversial topics; only she didn't tackle them as a journalist, she examined her subject as person. It was her plain-spoken empathy that audiences loved. She didn't sound like a college professor; she sounded like one of us.

In the mid-80s, Talk Talk released a string of solid radio hits that glowed with dazzling charm and wistful grace. In 1984, if you were speeding down Pacific Coast Highway in a convertible Porsche, Talk Talk's "It's My Life" would be blasting from your speakers. At the end of the decade, Talk Talk changed directions and released their experimental album, *Spirit of Eden*. With six minute plus reflective ballads and lyrics that delved into emotional black holes, Talk Talk's experimental album was met with confusion like watching Chainsaw and Dave try to graduate high school. While some fans bolted, others were intrigued by the empathetic soulfulness of Talk Talk's bold undertaking. Their free jazz, cerebral pop connected with their audience, inspiring the likes of Radiohead, Weezer, and Oasis.

Albums of the '80s:

The Party's Over (1982)
It's My Life (1984)
The Colour of Spring (1986)
Spirit of Eden (1988)

The 11 Best Songs By Talk Talk:

1. **It's My Life** (*It's My Life*)
2. **Talk Talk** (*The Party's Over*)
3. **Such A Shame** (*It's My Life*)
4. **Living In Another World** (*The Colour Of Spring*)
5. **Another Word** (*The Party's Over*)
6. **Eden** (*The Spirit of Eden*)
7. **Today** (*The Party's Over*)
8. **I Believe In You** (*The Spirit of Eden*)
9. **I Don't Believe in You** (*The Colour Of Spring*)
10. **Mirror Man** (*The Party's Over*)
11. **It's You** (*It's My Life*)

Fun Fact: Since the songs on *The Spirit of Eden* were made through a series of impromptu, instrumental jams, the band didn't think they could replicate the songs properly live. The band didn't tour in support of the album and broke up shortly after the release.

Song Note (Talk Talk): This song is about the lack of communication in society.

TALKING HEADS

Concert films are a rare art. There are hundreds of concert films, but only a handful have been strong enough to deserve a theatrical release. The film that all other concert films are compared to is The Talking Head's *Stop Making Sense*. The film is more than a concert film; it's the construction of a concert film, which unfolds right before your eyes and ears. The movie opens on lead singer, David Byrne, standing alone on a bare-bones stage with nothing except for a guitar, a microphone, and a boombox. He rips through an acoustic version of "Psycho Killer" where the spectacle is in the simplistic quality of his performance. As each successive song is played, the band adds more members, more set decoration, more complicated lighting, and finally climaxing in a finale with David Byrne wearing his iconic super-sized suit. By sharing the concert building experience, when we reach the full-blown finale, we feel more personally connected to the music and the band. *Stop Making Sense* is a symbolic representation of the music of the '80s. Though many '80s songs were covered in a sugary blanket of production, underneath all the loud colors and big hair were real songs with intimate human emotion. The Talking Heads understood that music needs a foundation of humanity to connect with its audience. If you strip away all the showy production and you have nothing there then you have nothing there. At the core of '80s pop, there was always something there. That's why decades later, those seemingly mindless songs still fondly stay in our hearts.

Albums of the '80s:

Remain in Light (1980)
Speaking In Tongues (1983)
Little Creatures (1985)
True Stories (1986)
Naked (1988)

The 11 Best Songs By The Talking Heads:

1. **Wild Wild Life** (*True Stories*)
2. **Once In A Lifetime** (*Remain in Light*)
3. **This Must Be The Place** (*Speaking In Tongues*)
4. **And She Was** (*Little Creatures*)
5. **Road To Nowhere** (*Little Creatures*)
6. **Girlfriend Is Better** (*Speaking In Tongues*)
7. **Crosseyed and Painless** (*Remain in Light*)
8. **City of Dreams** (*True Stories*)
9. **Stay Up Late** (*Little Creatures*)
10. **Perfect World** (*Little Creatures*)
11. **Burning Down The House** (*Speaking In Tongues*)

Fun Fact: Three band members, David Byrne, Tina Weymouth, and Chris Frantz all met in college at the Rhode Island School of Design. They met Jerry Harrison after they left school; Jerry was busy getting his college degree from Harvard.

TEARS FOR FEARS

Commercials used to be a necessary nuisance. They would interrupt our favorite TV show to sell us something useless like a Flowbee or a calculator watch. We accepted them because we didn't have a choice. Then, advertisers got creative and made commercials that were more engaging than the shows that they were interrupting. Commercials had adorable mascots like Spuds McKenzie the dog who loved beer or the Noid who hated pizza. We learned that Bo Jackson knew everything, the Energizer Bunny would never stop going, how to get a little closer, how to kiss a little longer, and how to get zestfully clean. When Wendy's slogan, "Where's the beef?" was introduced, it became a national phenomenon. In modern terms, it went viral. Commercials had become entertainment.

Tears For Fears had a similar breakout success. They were the first band of the synthpop, new wave genre to truly explode all over the mainstream. Their album *Songs From the Big Chair* went to number one on the Billboard charts, spawned two number one hits and sold over five million copies. The significance of this was a resonating changing of the guards. Tears For Fears had officially ushered in the '80s sound while closing the door on the '70s era. Tears for Fears was the band that solidified what the '80s were and what they would be remembered for. Up until then, the new wave culture still hovered in the shadows but now, with a grand shout they came out to rule the world.

Albums of the '80s:

The Hurting (1983)
Songs From The Big Chair (1985)
The Seeds Of Love (1989)

The 11 Best Songs By Tears For Fears:

1. **Everybody Wants To Rule The World** (*Songs From The Big Chair*)
2. **Head Over Heels** (*Songs From The Big Chair*)
3. **Mad World** (*The Hurting*)
4. **Change** (*The Hurting*)
5. **Watch Me Bleed** (*The Hurting*)
6. **Pale Shelter** (*The Hurting*)
7. **Shout** (*Songs From The Big Chair*)
8. **Sowing The Seeds Of Love** (*The Seeds Of Love*)
9. **Mothers Talk** (*Songs From The Big Chair*)
10. **The Way You Are** (*The Way You Are*)
11. **Year of the Knife** (*The Seeds of Love*)

Fun Fact: The name for the album, *Songs From The Big Chair*, was inspired by the movie, *Sybil*, where a young woman with multiple personalities, finds safety in a psychiatrist's chair.

Song Note (Shout): The song is based on Arthur Janov's Primal Therapy, where people deal with their fears by shouting as loud as they can.

THE THOMPSON TWINS

Fashion in the '80s wasn't defined by the type of clothes that you wore; it was defined by the way you wore them. Our jeans had to be stone-washed and pegged at the bottom. You couldn't have the peg too low, or you'd look like you were wearing bellbottoms, and if you had it too high, then it would look like you were digging for clams. You had to have them just high enough above your slip-on sneakers for everyone to know you weren't wearing socks. If you really wanted to look nice, the fashion-forward wore two Polo shirts with their jean jackets. And if you were going out to a club to celebrate '80s night, then you needed to have the big shoulder pads under your pastel jacket and matching cotton pants, accompanied by a keyboard tie (∞). MTV created a world where being judged by your looks was the norm; so our style had to speak volumes. We took our fashion cues from our rock heroes. The Thompson Twins weren't just trendsetters, they were the trend. From plaid linen pants to oversized suit jackets and hats that never matched, The Thompson Twins' loud and colorful fashion style appeared erratic but had a playful jubilance that transcended into their music. They made big pop songs with catchy hooks that you weren't annoyed by when they got stuck in your head. They made atmospheric themes for those car rides home from a party when all your friends just wanted to keep the joyous times flowing. Though their songs had colorful melodies on the surface, underneath, they had substance that gave credibility to their style.

Albums of the '80s:

A Product Of… (Participation) (1981)
Set/In the Name Of Love (1982)
Quick Step and Side Kick/Side Kicks (1983)
Into The Gap (1984)
Here's To Future Days (1985)
Close To The Bone (1987)
Big Trash (1989)

The 11 Best Songs By The Thompson Twins:

1. **Hold Me Now** (*Into The Gap*)
2. **If You Were Here** (*Quick Step and Side Kicks*)
3. **Lies** (*Quick Step and Side Kicks*)
4. **Doctor, Doctor** (*Into The Gap*)
5. **Long Goodbye** (*Close To The Bone*)
6. **King For A Day** (*Here's To Future Days*)
7. **Sister of Mercy** (*Into The Gap*)
8. **Savage Moon** (*Close To The Bone*)
9. **No Peace For The Wicked** (*Into The Gap*)
10. **Lay Your Hands On Me** (*Here's To Future Days*)
11. **When I See You** (*A Product Of…*)

Fun Fact: The band is named after the bumbling detectives from the *Adventures of Tintin* comic, Thomson and Thompson.

(∞) **80s Note:** A keyboard tie is a tie that looks like a piano keyboard.

'TIL TUESDAY

Fashion in the '80s wasn't defined by the style of clothes that you wore; it was defined by the company that made the clothes you wore. Did your shirt have a Lacoste alligator or a Polo player on it? Did you take off your Rayban sunglasses when you walked into a room or were they Vuarnet? Did you wear your Jordache jeans to a party or did you save up for months to buy a pair of Guess jeans? With minimum wage at a meager $3.35 per hour, it would take a week's salary to afford a pair of Guess jeans in hopes of looking as good as Claudia Schiffer or Naomi Campbell. We had to do it. We were defined by our brands. Were you an Esprit or Benetton girl? Were you a Vans or Airwalk guy? The brands you wore said more about who you were than you could say yourself.

'Til Tuesday embraced the '80s style without succumbing to it. The band held back from diving into the rainbow-laced pop bonanza and instead, elegant songs with pools of emotional volume. 'Til Tuesday brought introspection to an era dripping with superficiality. It's no wonder that when alt-rock obliterated the music industry, lead singer, Aimee Mann was one of the few '80s stalwarts to be able to reinvent herself as a '90s grunge siren. Unfortunately, to make the transition, she did trade in her electrified new wave hairdo for the unwashed grunge look. Besides that, 'Til Tuesday proves if you bring substance to your music, it doesn't matter what clothes you wear.

Albums of the '80s:

Voices Carry (1985)
Welcome Home (1986)
Everything's Different Now (1988)

The 11 Best Songs By 'Til Tuesday:

1. **Voices Carry** (*Voices Carry*)
2. **No More Crying** (*Voices Carry*)
3. **(Believed You Were) Lucky** (*Everything's Different Now*)
4. **Winning the War** (*Voices Carry*)
5. **Long Gone Buddy** (*Everything's Different Now*)
6. **Looking Over My Shoulder** (*Voices Carry*)
7. **Will She Just Fall Down** (*Welcome Home*)
8. **How Can You Give Up** (*Everything's Different Now*)
9. **Lover's Day** (*Welcome Home*)
10. **Love in a Vacuum** (*Voices Carry*)
11. **On Sunday** (*Welcome Home*)

Fun Fact: 'Til Tuesday's big breakout came by winning a Battle of the Bands radio contest on Boston's WBCN. They won with the song, "Love in A Vacuum," which they would go on to re-record for their debut album.

Song Note (Voices Carry): The video is inspired by a scene in the 1956 Alfred Hitchcock film, *The Man Who Knew Too Much*, where Doris Day screams in the middle of a symphony performance in order to thwart a murder.

TOTO

Before you go into a flurry of head scratching and eye rolling at the inclusion of Toto, I will vehemently support that the members of Toto may be the most important musicians of the '80s and by the end of this page, you will, too. Most people know Toto as the band who was obsessed with Roseanna Arquette and the weather conditions on the continent of Africa but in reality Toto's band members are the most prolific session musicians of the decade, if not of all time. Guitarist Steve Lukather has been featured as a session guitarist on over 1,500 recordings. He has helped Stevie Nicks stand back, Olivia Newton John get physical, Earth Wind & Fire boogie into wonderland, and Lionel Richie dance on the ceiling all night long. He has recorded with Aretha Franklin, Cheap Trick, Cher, Don Henley, Elton John, Joni Mitchell, Kiss, Ozzy Osbourne, and Van Halen. But he's not the only one. Drummer Jeff Porcaro has beat the skins on Pink Floyd's *The Wall*, multiple Steely Dan albums, and Madonna's *Like A Prayer*. Keyboardist David Paich and Steve Porcaro have played with the Doobie Brothers, Yes, Quincy Jones, and Diana Ross. The band's crowning achievement was recording for Michael Jackson's *Thriller*. Four members of Toto performed on a majority of the songs on the album. So if you ever wondered what Toto would sound like with Michael Jackson singing, now you know! If you combined all the album sales of all their appearances, you would have over 1 billion in sales. Not even the Beatles can say that. Now do you believe me?

Albums of the '80s:

Turn Back (1981)
Toto IV (1982)
Dune Soundtrack (1984)
Isolation (1984)
Fahrenheit (1986)
The Seventh One (1988)

The 11 Best Songs By Toto:

1. **Africa** (*IV*)
2. **Afraid of Love** (*IV*)
3. **Stranger In Town** (*Isolation*)
4. **Turn Back** (*Turn Back*)
5. **It's A Feeling** (*IV*)
6. **Gift With A Golden Gun** (*Turn Back*)
7. **Lovers In The Night** (*IV*)
8. **Rosanna** (*IV*)
9. **Goodbye Elenore** (*Turn Back*)
10. **Only The Children** (*The Seventh One*)
11. **English Eyes** (*Turn Back*)

Fun Fact: Toto performed the soundtrack to the movie *Dune*. Even though director David Lynch had the Police's frontman Sting starring in the movie, Lynch felt Toto would be the perfect band to accompany his sci-fi epic about spice worms, floating fat men, and a collection of cold sores.

U2

The door to my youth officially closed on October 21, 2015 when I was forced to accept that the promises made in *Back To The Future Part II* were not going to come true. The '80s were a time of limited technology. Sure, we had home computers, but they were very expensive and more of a novelty. I mean, you couldn't even go on the internet yet. All you could do was to type up essays and play video games made completely of words. That's right... no graphics, just words. When we saw the visionary future of 2015, our fertile young minds were sparked by the promises of flying cars, auto-lacing shoes, and hover boards. Skateboarding was my life, so the movie's prediction of a flying skateboard was a pipe dream (or half pipe dream) that was too good to be true. Though the 2015 music scene wasn't explored in the film, there would be one band from the '80s that would still be an icon thirty years later. That band is U2. U2 has made a career of reinventing themselves. They've done it so many times that they came all the way back to where they were in the first place. From the renegade fueled rebellion of *War* to the grandiose orpheum of *The Joshua Tree* to the bayou bar blues of *Rattle and Hum*, U2 was the zenith of American rock. They pondered, fought, questioned, praised and unified. They immortalized Dr. Martin Luther King in song and dedicated an entire album to the beauty of the American landscape. They celebrated our musical legends, jamming with BB King and Bob Dylan. They were the patriotic leaders we needed.

Albums of the '80s:

Boy (1980)
October (1981)
War (1983)
Wide Awake In America (1985)
The Unforgettable Fire (1984)
Joshua Tree (1987)
Rattle And Hum (1988)

The 11 Best Songs By U2:

1. **New Year's Day** (*War*)
2. **I Will Follow** (*Boy*)
3. **Like A Song...** (*War*)
4. **Pride** (*The Unforgettable Fire*)
5. **With Or Without You** (*The Joshua Tree*)
6. **Where The Streets Have No Name** (*The Joshua Tree*)
7. **The Unforgettable Fire** (*The Unforgettable Fire*)
8. **Out Of Control** (*Boy*)
9. **Sunday Bloody Sunday** (*War*)
10. **Stories For Boys** (*Boy*)
11. **Two Hearts Beat As One** (*War*)

Fun Fact: U2 became a band before they even knew how to play instruments. They were so bad when they started; they had no choice but to write their own songs because they weren't good enough to cover other people's music.

VAN HALEN

If you think the Transformers were the only robot toys that turned into cars and planes, you'll be stoked to know there's more than meets the eye. In the '80s, there was another line of transforming robots. They were called the Gobots. At the time, the Gobots and the Transformers were formidable opponents. Both toy lines had cool cars and planes that turned into robots. Both lines even had their own animated TV series. Ultimately, the Transformers won when their company bought the rights to the Gobots, basically erasing their existence. In the 2010s, after a long series of movies, the Transformers became the top dogs, and the Gobots were lost to the pages of history.

The other big rivalry in the '80s was between the two lead singers of Van Halen: David Lee Roth and Sammy Hagar. There was a conceit that you were either on Team David or Team Sammy. The biggest voice shouting that both sides were equal was likely from Team Sammy because Team David was too busy enjoying single life to care. Ultimately, when the Van Halen reunion with David Lee Roth came around, Sammy Hagar's tenure with the band was lost to history. Sammy Hagar did manage to procure a handful of successful Van Halen songs that made it possible to even have a discussion that there ever was a rivalry. Meanwhile, Gary Cherone is outside playing with his Machine Robos waiting for Michael Anthony to return his call.

Albums of the '80s:

Women And Children First (1980)
Fair Warning (1981)
Diver Down (1982)
1984 (1984)

The 11 Best Songs By David Lee Roth's Van Halen:

1. **Panama** (*1984*)
2. **Unchained** (*Fair Warning*)
3. **Hot For Teacher** (*1984*)
4. **Mean Street** (*Fair Warning*)
5. **Jump** (*1984*)
6. **Everybody Wants Some!!!** (*Women and Children First*)
7. **Little Guitars** (*Diver Down*)
8. **I'll Wait** (*1984*)
9. **...And The Cradle Will Rock** (*Women and Children First*)
10. **Secrets** (*Diver Down*)
11. **Take Your Whiskey Home** (*Women and Children First*)

Fun Fact: After seeing them play live, Gene Simmons of Kiss became a champion of the band. He set-up their first recording session and shopped their demo. The band was rejected on first listen because disco was "in" and rock was on the way "out."

WHITESNAKE

Even though Whitesnake is largely considered a hair-driven metal band, they originally formed out of the ashes of the seminal '70s rock band, Deep Purple. Whitesnake hit superstardom on their 1987 self-titled release, which shed many of their guitar jams in lieu of straightforward, glossy, rock radio venom. They were so determined that they even re-recorded a handful of their blues songs as rock glam gold. It was hard to argue with their musical evolution (or de-evolution, depending who you ask) when their self-titled album went on to sell 8 million copies. But their success may not come down to their musical re-branding effort. There may be another reason... and her name is Tawny Kitaen. In Whitesnake's video for "Here I Go Again," Tawny Kitaen is featured in a white negligee, writhing in a seductive dance on the hoods of two Jaguar cars. The sexual energy in the video was so magnetic; it was practically impossible for a teenage boy to turn away from the video once it started. Tawny represented the allure of the rock star lifestyle. Having a woman like her became every metal band's dream. That includes Whitesnake's lead singer, David Coverdale, who would go on to marry Tawny, that is until she cheated on him with all people: OJ Simpson (while he was still married to Nicole Brown). This was not the love David Coverdale was feeling, so he left Tawny in the still of the night because he wouldn't be a fool for her loving no more.

Albums of the '80s:

Ready an' Willing (1980)
Come an' Get It (1981)
Saints & Sinners (1982)
Slide It In (1984)
Whitesnake (1987)
Slip of the Tongue (1989)

The 11 Best Songs By Whitesnake:

1. **Here I Go Again** (*Whitesnake*)
2. **Don't Break My Heart Again** (*Come An' Get It*)
3. **Standing in the Shadow** (*Slide It In*)
4. **Fool for Your Loving** (*Ready an' Willing*)
5. **Love Ain't No Stranger** (*Slide It In*)
6. **Crying In the Rain** (*Saints & Sinners*)
7. **Is This Love?** (*Whitesnake*)
8. **Ain't Gonna To Cry No More** (*Ready an' Willing*)
9. **Give Me All Your Love Tonight** (*Whitesnake*)
10. **Ready an' Willing** (*Ready an' Willing*)
11. **Still of The Night** (*Whitesnake*)

Fun Fact: When the 1987 self-titled album was released, the guitarist, bassist, and drummer all the left the band. Lead singer, David Coverdale, had to assemble a new band to go out and tour in support of the album.

*H*TC

What made the '80s music so important was the introduction of so many genres. We heard the explosion of metal, goth, rap, new wave, even the birth of electronica. While punk thrived in the '80s, it struggled to maintain its footing. The first wave of punk rock came out of nowhere and scorched the earth with the rebellious screams of disgruntled youth. Punk came into our lives scalding hot and burned out as fast as it arrived, leaving a new crop of angry bands in its wake. Punk became fractured as a new genre took form: the post-punks. XTC was born out of the post-punk movement. Post-punks were bands that held tight to the punk ideology, but their musical concoctions were too eclectic to get a membership to any other genre. XTC, who carried a '60s psychedelic sound, were too poppy to be punk but too punk to be pop. Falling into that grey area in between, XTC and the other post-punk bands laid the foundation for alternative rock. Outside of *120 Minutes* and some college radio stations, XTC was limited in their popularity. XTC was a studio-only band. They didn't tour. They couldn't tour. Lead singer, Andy Partridge, came down with debilitating stage fright before a show at the Hollywood Palladium and never toured again. They had to rely solely on radio play for people to even know they existed. This created a mythos about the band. They were like an amusement park that was never open. They did gain a cult following but were ultimately limited in their exposure. XTC represents all the unique '80s facets that could have been but never were.

Albums of the '80s:

Black Sea (1980)
English Settlement (1982)
Mummer (1983)
The Big Express (1984)
Skylarking (1986)
Oranges & Lemons (1989)

The 11 Best Songs By XTC:

1. **Dear God** (*Skylarking*)
2. **Earn Enough For Us** (*Skylarking*)
3. **Towers of London** (*Black Sea*)
4. **The Mayor of Simpleton** (*Oranges & Lemons*)
5. **Senses Working Overtime** (*English Settlement*)
6. **Funk Pop A Roll** (*Mummer*)
7. **Generals and Majors** (*Black Sea*)
8. **Respectable Street** (*Black Sea*)
9. **This World Over** (*The Big Express*)
10. **Garden of Earthly Delights** (*Oranges & Lemons*)
11. **Ball and Chain** (*English Settlement*)

Fun Fact: Their album, *Skylarking*, was produced by Todd Rundgen. Andy Partridge wanted to produce the album himself, but the record label wanted another producer to oversee the process. Because Rundgren was an uninvited guest of the band, it made the recording process unbearable and lengthy. Rundgren says it was one of the worst experiences of his long career.

1980

Big Music Events of 1980:

Ron Wood of The Rolling Stones is arrested in the Caribbean for cocaine possession. Paul McCartney is arrested in Tokyo for marijuana possession. Don Henley is arrested for marijuana *and* cocaine possession. The first rock festival in Russia takes place. The first Monsters of Rock concert debuts in Donington Park, UK. Brian Johnson becomes the new singer of AC/DC. Ronnie James Dio becomes the new singer of Black Sabbath. The Sony Walkman debuts. The Eagles, Germs, Led Zeppelin, Uriah Heep, and Wire break up.

The 11 Best-Selling Albums of 1980:

1. Pink Floyd - *The Wall*
2. The Eagles - *The Long Run*
3. Michael Jackson - *Off the Wall*
4. Billy Joel - *Glass Houses*
5. Tom Petty and The Heartbreakers - *Damn The Torpedoes*
6. Bob Seger & the Silver Bullet Band - *Against The Wind*
7. Pat Benatar - *In The Heat Of The Night*
8. Blondie - *Eat To The Beat*
9. Led Zeppelin - *In Through The Out Door*
10. Kenny Rogers - *Kenny*
11. Kool & The Gang - *Ladies Night*

Hit Songs:

- "Another Brick In The Wall" - Pink Floyd
- "Call Me" - Blondie
- "Magic" - Olivia Newton-John
- "Rock With You" - Michael Jackson
- "Do That To Me One More Time" - Captain & Tenille
- "Crazy Little Thing Called Love" - Queen
- "Funkytown" - Lipps, Inc.
- "Cars" - Gary Numan
- "It's Still Rock And Roll To Me" - Billy Joel
- "Sailing" - Christopher Cross
- "Coward Of The County" - Kenny Rogers
- "Against The Wind" - Bob Seger & Silver Bullet Band
- "Fame" - Irene Cara
- "Off The Wall" - Michael Jackson
- "Tusk" - Fleetwood Mac
- "Refugee" - Tom Petty and the Heartbreakers
- "Heartbreaker" - Pat Benatar

R.I.P.:

Jimmy Durante
Bon Scott (AC/DC)
Ian Curtis (Joy Division)
Keith Godchaux (Grateful Dead)
John Bonham (Led Zeppelin)
John Lennon (The Beatles)

1981

Big Music Events of 1981:

Ozzy Osbourne bites the head off a dove. Diana Ross signs the most lucrative record deal of all time for $20 million. Kerrang! magazine publishes its first issue. MTV premieres, making music a potent visual medium. Around 35 million people watch a live satellite broadcast of a Rod Stewart concert. Simon & Garfunkel reunite and give a free concert in New York's Central Park. Only 500,000 people show up because everyone else is home watching MTV. Steely Dan, Wings, and Yes break-up.

The 11 Best-Selling Albums of 1981:

1. REO Speedwagon - *Hi Infidelity*
2. John Lennon & Yoko Ono - *Double Fantasy*
3. Kenny Rogers - *Greatest Hits*
4. Christopher Cross - *Christopher Cross*
5. Pat Benatar - *Crimes of Passion*
6. Styx - *Paradise Theater*
7. AC/DC - *Back in Black*
8. Hall & Oates - *Voices*
9. The Police - *Zenyatta Mondatta*
10. Bruce Springsteen - *The River*
11. The Alan Parsons Project - *The Turn Of A Friendly Card*

Hit Songs:

- "Bette Davis Eyes" - Kim Carnes
- "Endless Love" - Diana Ross and Lionel Richie
- "Lady" - Kenny Rogers
- "Jessie's Girl" - Rick Springfield
- "Celebration" - Kool and the Gang
- "Kiss On My List" - Hall & Oates
- "9 to 5" - Dolly Parton
- "Elvira" - Oak Ridge Boys
- "Keep on Loving You" - REO Speedwagon
- "Hit Me With Your Best Shot" - Pat Benatar
- "America" - Neil Diamond
- "Whip It" - Devo
- "Shook Me All Night Long" - AC/DC

R.I.P.:

Bill Haley

Bob Hite (Canned Heat)

Bob Marley

Rushton Moreve (Steppenwolf)

Harry Chapin

Steve Currie (T. Rex)

1982

Big Music Events of 1982:

Ozzy Osbourne has an encore performance of eating flying animals and bites the head off a bat. Ozzy marries his manager, Sharon; starts planning a TV show. BB King donates 7,000 blues records to the University of Mississippi. Christians protest Iron Maiden's *Number of the Beast* by buying the album then burning it, not understanding how protests work. Compact Discs go on sale. Madonna debuts. ABBA, Blondie, Captain Beefheart, The Doobie Brothers, The Jam, Squeeze, and The Who break-up.

The 11 Best-Selling Albums of 1982:

1. Asia - *Asia*
2. The Go-Gos - *Beauty and the Beat*
3. Foreigner - *4*
4. John Cougar - *American Fool*
5. J. Geils Band - *Freeze Frame*
6. Journey - *Escape*
7. Loverboy - *Get Lucky*
8. Stevie Nicks - *Bella Donna*
9. Vangelis - *Chariots of Fire*
10. The Police - *Ghost In The Machine*
11. The Rolling Stones - *Tattoo You*

Hit Songs:

- "867-5309 (Jenny)" - Tommy Tutone
- "Abracadabra" - Steve Miller Band
- "Arthur's Theme" - Christopher Cross
- "Caught Up In You" - .38 Special
- "Centerfold" - J. Geils Band
- "Chariots of Fire" - Vangelis
- "Ebony and Ivory" Paul McCartney and Stevie Wonder
- "Eye of the Tiger" - Survivor
- "Gloria" - Laura Branigan
- "Heat of the Moment" - Asia
- "Jack and Diane" - John Cougar
- "Kids In America" - Kim Wilde
- "Open Arms" - Journey
- "Pac-Man Fever" - Buckner & Garcia
- "Physical" - Olivia Newton-John
- "Tainted Love" - Soft Cell
- "Working For The Weekend" - Loverboy

R.I.P.:

Lightnin' Hopkins

John Belushi (The Blues Brothers)

Randy Rhoades (Quiet Riot/Ozzy Osbourne)

Lester Bangs (music critic)

James Honeyman-Scott (The Pretenders)

Joe Tex

1983

Big Music Events of 1983:

Michael Jackson's *Thriller* is #1 on the charts for 37 weeks. His video of the same name debuts and stands as the greatest music video of all time. Dave Mustaine is fired from Metallica; forms Megadeth. *Friday Night Videos* premieres on NBC. Quiet Riot's *Metal Health* is the first metal album to hit #1 on the charts. Kiss appear on MTV without their signature makeup for the first time. Marvin Gaye buys his dad a gun for Christmas (spoiler alert). The Carpenters, Gang of Four, Humble Pie, Misfits, Roxy Music, Simon & Garfunkel, and Sly & The Family Stone all break-up.

The 11 Best-Selling Albums of 1983:

1. Michael Jackson - *Thriller*
2. Men At Work - *Business As Usual*
3. The Police - *Synchronicity*
4. Hall & Oates - *H20*
5. Prince & The Revolution - *1999*
6. Lionel Richie - *Lionel Richie*
7. Jane Fonda - *Jane Fonda's Workout Record*
8. Def Leppard - *Pyromania*
9. Culture Club - *Kissing To Be Clever*
10. Olivia Newton-John - *Greatest Hits Vol. 2*
11. Toto - *Toto IV*

Hit Songs:

- "Beat It" - Michael Jackson
- "Billie Jean" - Michael Jackson
- "Come On Eileen" - Dexys Midnight Runners
- "Do You Really Want To Hurt Me" - Culture Club
- "Down Under" - Men At Work
- "Electric Avenue" - Eddy Grant
- "Every Breath You Take" - Police
- "Flashdance...What A Feeling" - Irene Cara
- "Maniac" - Michael Sembello
- "Mickey" - Toni Basil
- "Mr. Roboto" - Styx
- "The Safety Dance" - Men Without Hats
- "Sexual Healing" - Marvin Gaye
- "Sweet Dreams (Are Made Of This)" - Eurythmics
- "Thriller" - Michael Jackson
- "Total Eclipse Of The Heart" - Bonnie Tyler
- "True" - Spandau Ballet

R.I.P.:

Karen Carpenter (The Carpenters)

Pete Farndon (The Pretenders)

Felix Pappalardi (Mountain)

Muddy Waters

Chris Wood (Traffic)

Tom Evans (Badfinger)

Dennis Wilson (The Beach Boys)

1984

Big Music Events of 1984:

BBC bans the song "Relax" by Frankie Goes To Hollywood (song still goes to #1). Pepsi Cola sets Michael Jackson's hair on fire; he begins drinking 7-Up. The MTV Video Music Awards debut; Herbie Hancock is the top winner. Bruce Springsteen's *Born in the U.S.A.* is the first CD made in America. Band Aid records their charity single, "Do They Know It's Christmas?" Def Leppard drummer, Rick Allen, loses his arm... keeps drumming. Tipper Gore forms the P.M.R.C. after hearing Prince's *Purple Rain*. Kansas, King Crimson, Rainbow, Split Enz, Styx, and Thin Lizzy break-up.

The 11 Best-Selling Albums of 1984

1. Michael Jackson - *Thriller*
2. Huey Lewis and The News - *Sports*
3. Lionel Richie - *Can't Slow Down*
4. Billy Joel - *An Innocent Man*
5. Culture Club - *Colour By Numbers*
6. Van Halen - *1984*
7. ZZ Top - *Eliminator*
8. The Police - *Synchronicity*
9. Footloose Soundtrack
10. Duran Duran - *Seven And The Ragged Tiger*
11. Cyndi Lauper - *She's So Unusual*

Hit Songs:

- "99 Luft Balloons" - Nena
- "Borderline" - Madonna
- "Cum On Feel The Noize" - Quiet Riot
- "Footloose" - Kenny Loggins
- "Ghostbusters" - Ray Parker Jr.
- "Girls Just Want To Have Fun" - Cyndi Lauper
- "The Heart of Rock & Roll" - Huey Lewis and The News
- "Hello" - Lionel Richie
- "Islands In the Stream" - Kenny Rogers and Dolly Parton
- "Karma Chameleon" - Culture Club
- "Legs" - ZZ Top
- "Relax" - Frankie Goes To Hollywood
- "Round and Round" - Ratt
- "Say Say Say" - Paul McCartney and Michael Jackson
- "Somebody's Watching Me" - Rockwell
- "Uptown Girl" - Billy Joel
- "What's Love Got To Do With It" - Tina Turner
- "When Doves Cry" - Prince

R.I.P.:

Jackie Wilson
Marvin Gaye
Count Basie
Razzle (Hanoi Rocks)

1985

Big Music Events of 1985:

VH-1 premieres. USA for Africa records a charity single to stop famine in Africa because we can't let the Brits win. David Lee Roth quits Van Halen. Wham! is the first Western band to perform in China. They do it again an hour later. Live Aid takes place, every band ever performs. Farm Aid takes place (the country version of Live Aid). Michael Jackson outbids Paul McCartney; buys rights to the Beatles music. Judas Priest is sued when two young fans commit suicide after listening to the band's music. Kajagoogoo and The Minutemen break-up.

The 11 Best-Selling Albums of 1985:

1. Bruce Springsteen - *Born In The USA*
2. Bryan Adams - *Reckless*
3. Madonna - *Like A Virgin*
4. Wham! - *Make It Big*
5. Tina Turner - *Private Dancer*
6. Phil Collins - *No Jacket Required*
7. *Beverly Hills Cop Soundtrack*
8. Billy Ocean - *Suddenly*
9. Prince & The Revolution - *Purple Rain*
10. Tears For Fears - *Songs From The Big Chair*
11. John Fogerty - *Centerfield*

Hit Songs:

- "Axel F" - Harold Faltermeyer
- "California Girls" - David Lee Roth
- "Can't Fight This Feeling" - REO Speedwagon
- "Cool It Now" - New Edition
- "Don't You (Forget About Me)" - Simple Minds
- "I Feel For You" - Chaka Khan
- "I Want To Know What Love Is" - Foreigner
- "Like A Virgin" - Madonna
- "Miami Vice Theme" - Jan Hammer
- "Money For Nothing" - Dire Straits
- "Part-Time Lover" - Stevie Wonder
- "Sea Of Love" - The Honeydrippers
- "Smooth Operator" - Sade
- "St. Elmo's Fire (Man In Motion)" - John Parr
- "Strut" - Sheena Easton
- "Summer of '69" - Bryan Adams
- "Wake Me Up Before You Go-Go" - Wham!
- "We Are The World" - USA For Africa
- "We Built This City" - Starship
- "We Don't Need Another Hero" - Tina Turner

R.I.P.:

David Byron (Uriah Heep)
Ricky Wilson (The B-52s)
D. Boon (The Minutemen)
Ricky Nelson

1986

Big Music Events of 1986:

Rock & Roll Hall of Fame holds its first-ever induction ceremony; Elvis Presley, Chuck Berry, Buddy Holly, Sam Cooke, James Brown and Jerry Lee Lewis are some of the first inductees. Metallica's tour bus crashes, killing their bassist, Cliff Burton. Asia, Black Flag, The Clash, Dead Kennedys, ELO, Men At Work, and Wham! all break-up.

The 11 Best-Selling Albums of 1986:

1. Whitney Houston - *Whitney Houston*
2. Heart - *Heart*
3. John Cougar Mellencamp - *Scarecrow*
4. ZZ Top - *Afterburner*
5. Dire Straits - *Brothers In Arms*
6. Janet Jackson - *Control*
7. Mr. Mister - *Welcome To The Real World*
8. Sade - *Promise*
9. Phil Collins - *No Jacket Required*
10. Miami Sound Machine - *Primitive Love*
11. Robert Palmer - *Riptide*

Hit Songs:

- "Addicted To Love" - Robert Palmer
- "Broken Wings" - Mr. Mister
- "Conga" - Miami Sound Machine
- "Dancing On The Ceiling" - Lionel Richie
- "Danger Zone" - Kenny Loggins
- "Living In America" - James Brown
- "Party All The Time" - Eddie Murphy
- "R.O.C.K. in the U.S.A." - John Cougar Mellencamp
- "Rock Me Amadeus" - Falco
- "Rumors" - Timex Social Club
- "Sledgehammer" - Peter Gabriel
- "Take Me Home Tonight" - Eddie Money
- "Take My Breath Away" - Berlin
- "Walk This Way" - Run D.M.C. and Aerosmith
- "West End Girls" - Pet Shop Boys
- "Who's Johnny" - El Debarge
- "Word Up!" - Cameo
- "You Give Love A Bad Name" - Bon Jovi
- "Your Love" - The Outfield

R.I.P.:

Phil Lynott (Thin Lizzy)
Richard Manuel (The Band)
O'Kelly Isley, Jr. (The Isley Brothers)
Benny Goodman
Cliff Burton (Metallica)

1987

Big Music Events of 1987:

Sonny Bono runs for mayor of Palm Springs (and wins). Beastie Boys are first artist censored by American Bandstand. Bryan Adams' song, "Heat of the Night" is first single released on cassette (called a Cassingle - although I've never heard that said out loud). Whitney Houston's second album, *Whitney*, is the first album by a woman to debut at #1. Glam metal band Alice N' Chains breaks up, one of their members, Layne Staley forms a new band called Alice in Chains. Hüsker Dü and The Smiths break-up.

The 11 Best-Selling Albums of 1987:

1. Bon Jovi - *Slippery When Wet*
2. Paul Simon - *Graceland*
3. Beastie Boys - *Licensed To Ill*
4. Bruce Hornsby and the Range - *The Way it Is*
5. Janet Jackson - *Control*
6. U2 - *The Joshua Tree*
7. Huey Lewis and the News - *Fore!*
8. Cinderella - *Night Songs*
9. Anita Baker - *Rapture*
10. Genesis - *Invisible Touch*
11. Madonna - *True Blue*

Hit Songs:

- "Alone" - Heart
- "Bad" - Michael Jackson
- "Control" - Janet Jackson
- "Don't Dream It's Over" - Crowded House
- "Everybody Have Fun Tonight" - Wang Chung
- "Heart and Soul" - T'Pau
- "(I Just) Died In Your Arms" - Cutting Crew
- "I Think We're Alone Now" - Tiffany
- "I Wanna Dance With Somebody" - Whitney Houston
- "La Bamba" - Los Lobos
- "Land of Confusion" - Genesis
- "Little Lies" - Fleetwood Mac
- "Livin' On A Prayer" - Bon Jovi
- "Looking For A New Love" - Jody Watley
- "Walk Like An Egyptian" - The Bangles
- "Fight For Your Right (To Party!)" - Beastie Boys

R.I.P.:

Liberace

Buddy Rich

Paul Butterfield

Gary Driscoll (Rainbow)

Fred Astaire

Scott La Rock (Boogie Down Productions)

Peter Tosh (The Wailers)

Jaco Pastorius

1988

Big Music Events of 1988:

Man claims to have secretly posed as Nikki Sixx of Mötley Crüe and toured with the band. Nikki Sixx does not claim to have secretly posed as the man. Led Zeppelin reunites with John Bonham's son, Jason Bonham, filling in on drums. Public Enemy plays a concert at Riker's Island Prison. James Brown takes police on wild chase because he couldn't find a bathroom. John Fogerty is accused of plagiarizing himself. The Cars, The dBs, and Mr. Mister break-up.

The 11 Best-Selling Albums of 1988:

1. George Michael - *Faith*
2. Dirty Dancing Soundtrack
3. Def Leppard - *Hysteria*
4. INXS - *Kick*
5. Michael Jackson - *Bad*
6. Guns N' Roses - *Appetite For Destruction*
7. Debbie Gibson - *Out of the Blue*
8. Richard Marx - *Richard Marx*
9. Tiffany - *Tiffany*
10. Aerosmith - *Permanent Vacation*
11. Terence Trent D'Arby - *The Hardline According To Terence Trent D'Arby*

Hit Songs:

- "Candle In The Wind" - Elton John
- "Don't Worry Be Happy" - Bobby McFerrin
- "Faith" - George Michael
- "Got My Mind Set On You" - George Harrison
- "Man In The Mirror" - Michael Jackson
- "Never Gonna Give You Up" - Rick Astley
- "Never Tear Us Apart" - INXS
- "Pour Some Sugar on Me" - Def Leppard
- "Red, Red Wine" - UB40
- "Shattered Dreams" - Johnny Hates Jazz
- "Simply Irresistible" - Robert Palmer
- "So Emotional" - Whitney Houston
- "Sweet Child O' Mine" - Guns N' Roses
- "What's On Your Mind" - Information Society

R.I.P.:

John Curulewski (Styx)

Memphis Slim

Andy Gibb (Bee Gees)

Dave Prater (Sam & Dave)

Chet Baker

Gil Evans

Hillel Slovak (Red Hot Chili Peppers)

Nico

Son House

Roy Orbison

1989

Big Music Events of 1989:

Madonna's religious-themed music video, "Like A Prayer," draws heavy criticism but may be her best song to date. Soul Train names Michael Jackson the King of Pop. The Monkees reunite for a one-off concert in Los Angeles. Ice Cube quits N.W.A. The Jackson Five disband.

The 11 Best-Selling Albums of 1989:

1. Bobby Brown - *Don't Be Cruel*
2. New Kids on the Block - *Hangin' Tough*
3. Paula Abdul - *Forever Your Girl*
4. Bon Jovi - *New Jersey*
5. Guns N' Roses - *Appetite For Destruction*
6. Fine Young Cannibals - *The Raw And The Cooked*
7. Guns N' Roses - *G'N'R Lies*
8. Traveling Wilburys - *Vol. 1*
9. Def Leppard - *Hysteria*
10. Milli Vanilli - *Girl, You Know It's True*
11. Skid Row - *Skid Row*

Hit Songs:

- "Buffalo Stance" - Nena Cherry
- "Bust A Move" - Young MC
- "Girl, You Know It's True" - Milli Vanilli
- "Hangin' Tough" - New Kids On The Block
- "If I Could Turn Back Time" - Cher
- "Like A Prayer" - Madonna
- "The Look" - Roxette
- "Love Shack" - The B-52s
- "My Prerogative - Bobby Brown
- "Patience" - Guns N' Roses
- "The Promise" - When In Rome
- "Smooth Criminal" - Michael Jackson
- "Stand" - REM
- "Straight Up" - Paula Abdul
- "Toy Soldiers" - Martika
- "Wild Thing" - Tone Lōc
- "Wind Beneath My Wings" - Bette Midler

R.I.P.:

Paul Robi (The Platters)

John Cipollina (Quicksilver Messenger Service)

Pete De Freitas (Echo & The Bunnymen)

Keith "Cowboy" Wiggins (Grandmaster Flash & The Furious Five)

Alan Murphy (Level 42)

Billy Lyall (Bay City Rollers, Pilot)

The Next Best III Albums of the 80s

In case you still haven't found enough music, here is a bonus list with some more great albums to keep you busy until my next book.

1. 10,000 Maniacs - *In My Tribe* (1987)
2. .38 Special - *Wild-Eyed Southern Boys* (1981)
3. 3rd Bass - *The Cactus Album* (1989)
4. A Flock of Seagulls - *A Flock of Seagulls* (1982)
5. A-Ha - *Hunting High and Low* (1985)
6. Bryan Adams - *Reckless* (1984)
7. Aerosmith - *Pump* (1989)
8. Altered Image - *Happy Birthday* (1981)
9. The Bangles - *All Over The Place* (1984)
10. Pat Benatar - *Get Nervous* (1982)
11. Black Sabbath - *Heaven and Hell* (1980)
12. Blondie - *Autoamerican* (1980)
13. Bon Jovi - *Slippery When Wet* (1986)
14. Boogie Down Productions - *By All Means Necessary* (1988)
15. David Bowie - *Scary Monsters (and Super Creeps)* (1980)
16. Kate Bush - *Hounds of Love* (1985)
17. The Clash - *Sandinista!* (1980)
18. Cocteau Twins - *Garlands* (1982)
19. Elvis Costello - *Imperial Bedroom* (1982)
20. Crowded House - *Crowded House* (1986)
21. The Cult - *Love* (1985)
22. Culture Club - *Colour By Numbers* (1983)

23. The Cure - *Head on The Door* (1985)
24. The Cure - *Pornography* (1982)
25. The dBs - *Stands for Decibels* (1981)
26. Def Leppard - *High 'N' Dry* (1981)
27. Depeche Mode - *Some Great Reward* (1984)
28. Dexys Midnight Runners - *Searching For The Young Soul Rebels* (1980)
29. Dinosaur Jr. - *You're Living All Over Me* (1987)
30. Dio - *Holy Diver* (1983)
31. Dire Straits - *Brothers in Arms* (1985)
32. Steve Earle - *Guitar Town* (1986)
33. Echo & The Bunnymen - *Porcupine* (1983)
34. EPMD - *Strictly Business* (1988)
35. The English Beat - *Special Beat Service* (1982)
36. John Fogerty - *Centerfield* (1985)
37. Foreigner - *4* (1981)
38. Gang Of Four - *Solid Gold* (1981)
39. General Public - *All The Rage* (1984)
40. The Go-Go's - *Beauty and the Beat* (1981)
41. Grandmaster Flash & The Furious Five - *The Message* (1982)
42. The Grateful Dead - *In The Dark* (1987)
43. Whitney Houston - *Whitney Houston* (1985)
44. Hüsker Dü - *New Day Rising* (1985)
45. Ice-T - *Rhyme Pays* (1987)
46. INXS - *Listen Like Thieves* (1985)
47. Iron Maiden - *Killers* (1981)
48. The Jacksons - *Triumph* (1980)
49. Jesus and The Mary Chain - *Darklands* (1987)
50. Joan Jett - *I Love Rock 'N' Roll* (1981)
51. Billy Joel - *Glass Houses* (1980)
52. Journey - *Frontiers* (1983)
53. Judas Priest - *Screaming for Vengeance* (1982)
54. Jungle Brothers - *Done By The Forces of Nature* (1989)

55. LL Cool J - *Walking With A Panther* (1989)
56. Cyndi Lauper - *She's So Unusual* (1984)
57. Led Zeppelin - *Coda* (1982)
58. Let's Active - *Cypress* (1984)
59. Love and Rockets - *Express* (1986)
60. Madness -*The Rise & Fall* (1982)
61. Madonna - *True Blue* (1986)
62. Bob Marley and the Wailers - *Uprising* (1980)
63. Meat Puppets - *II* (1984)
64. Megadeth - *Peace Sells...But Who's Buying?* (1986)
65. John Cougar Mellencamp - *Scarecrow* (1985)
66. Men At Work - *Business As Usual* (1981)
67. Metallica - *Ride The Lightning* (1984)
68. Metallica - *Master of Puppets* (1986)
69. George Michael - *Faith* (1987)
70. Midnight Oil - *Diesel and Dust* (1987)
71. Mötley Crüe - *Shout At the Devil* (1983)
72. Motörhead - *Ace of Spades* (1980)
73. My Bloody Valentine - *Isn't Anything* (1988)
74. New Order - *Technique* (1989)
75. Oingo Boingo - *Dead Man's Party* (1985)
76. O.M.D. - *Architecture and Morality* (1981)
77. Ozzy Osbourne - *Blizzard of Ozz* (1980)
78. Pet Shop Boys - *Please* (1986)
79. The Police - *The Ghost in the Machine* (1981)
80. Pretenders - *Learning To Crawl* (1984)
81. Psychedelic Furs - *Talk Talk Talk* (1981)
82. Queensrÿche - *Operation: Mindcrime* (1988)
83. Quiet Riot - *Metal Health* (1983)
84. Lou Reed - *The Blue Mask* (1982)
85. Lou Reed - *New York* (1989)
86. R.E.M. - *Reckoning* (1984)
87. R.E.M. - *Green* (1988)
88. Replacements - *Pleased To Meet Me* (1987)

89. Robbie Robertson - *Robbie Robertson* (1987)
90. Rolling Stones - *Tattoo You* (1981)
91. Roxette - *Look Sharp!* (1988)
92. Paul Simon - *Graceland* (1986)
93. Shalamar - *Friends* (1982)
94. Sisters of Mercy - *Floodland* (1987)
95. Slayer - *Reign In Blood* (1986)
96. The Smiths - *The Smiths* (1984)
97. The Smiths - *Strangeways, Here We Come* (1987)
98. The Soft Boys - *Underwater Moonlight* (1980)
99. Soundgarden - *Louder Than Love* (1989)
100. Rick Springfield - *Working Class Dog* (1981)
101. Bruce Springsteen - *Tunnel of Love* (1987)
102. Talking Heads - *Speaking in Tongues* (1983)
103. Toto - *IV* (1982)
104. Tina Turner - *Private Dancer* (1984)
105. U2 - *Rattle and Hum* (1988)
106. Ultramagnetic MCs - *Critical Beatdown* (1988)
107. Van Halen - *Fair Warning* (1981)
108. X - *Los Angeles* (1980)
109. XTC - *Skylarking* (1986)
110. Neil Young - *Freedom* (1989)
111. ZZ Top - *Eliminator* (1983)

Thank Yous

(in no particular order)

1. Stores in the mall (Sam Goody, Licorice Pizza, Wherehouse, Musicland, Camelot)
2. My Hometown Stores (Danny's Records-Fresno, Ragin' Records-Visalia, Velouria-Visalia)
3. LA Stores Then (Aron's Records, Moby Disc, Off-Beat, Penny Lane, Record Surplus, Rhino Records, Tower Records)
4. LA Stores Now (Amoeba Records, Atomic Records, CD Trader, Freak Beat, Touch Vinyl)
5. Radio Stations (KROQ, KNAC, KCRW, KXLU, KQLZ, KKDJ, KNDD, KITS)
6. Music Journals (Rolling Stone, CMJ, Mojo, Q, NME, Filter, Hit Parader, Circus, Kerrang!)
7. Music Videos (Headbangers Ball, 120 Minutes, Friday Night Videos, Yo! MTV Raps)
8. KLA (UCLA's Totally Awesome Radio Station)
9. CD Burners & Blank Cassettes
10. Internet (Napster, Emusic, Mp3s, Spotify, Stereogum, The Hype Machine)
11. My music friends who have never let me down, you know who you are

Printed in Great Britain
by Amazon

29067405R00160